ROADBLOCKS IN

D0153618

# Roadblocks in Acting

Rob Roznowski

© Rob Roznowski 2017

All rights reserved. No reproduction, copy or transmission of this publication may be made without written permission.

No portion of this publication may be reproduced, copied or transmitted save with written permission or in accordance with the provisions of the Copyright, Designs and Patents Act 1988, or under the terms of any licence permitting limited copying issued by the Copyright Licensing Agency, Saffron House, 6–10 Kirby Street, London EC1N 8TS.

Any person who does any unauthorized act in relation to this publication may be liable to criminal prosecution and civil claims for damages.

The author has asserted his right to be identified as the author of this work in accordance with the Copyright, Designs and Patents Act 1988.

First published 2017 by
PALGRAVE

Palgrave in the UK is an imprint of Macmillan Publishers Limited, registered in England, company number 785998, of 4 Crinan Street, London, N1 9XW.

Palgrave® and Macmillan® are registered trademarks in the United States, the United Kingdom, Europe and other countries.

ISBN 978–1–137–60987–8 hardback
ISBN 978–1–137–60986–1 paperback

This book is printed on paper suitable for recycling and made from fully managed and sustained forest sources. Logging, pulping and manufacturing processes are expected to conform to the environmental regulations of the country of origin.

A catalogue record for this book is available from the British Library.

A catalog record for this book is available from the Library of Congress.

Printed and bound by CPI Group (UK) Ltd, Croydon, CR0 4YY

*This book is dedicated to Sarah Goeke, my graduate research assistant on the book. Watching her overcome roadblocks in her acting was inspirational. It is also dedicated to the students and professional actors I have worked with during my time as a theater educator and artist. I am amazed daily by their bravery.*

# Contents

# List of Illustrations

## Figures

## Tables

# List of Exercises

# Testimonials

| | |
|---|---|
| Bonnie Bairley | Katherine Noyes |
| Carolyn Conover | Maddy Shammas |
| Elijah El | Mykayla Smith |
| Sarah Goeke | Kathryn Stahl |
| Matt Greenbaum | Margaret Turbett |
| Andrew Head | Andrew Van Otteren |
| Bethany Heinlein | |

Other actors whose work was offered in the book through written contributions, interview questions, or other means include:

Kristy Allen, Taylor Blair, Derek Bry, Lee Cleavland, Paige Conway, Jen English, Jonathan Hamilton, Grace Hinkley, Greg Hunter, Blaine Mizer, Jenna Pall, Kirill Shenyerman, Zev Steinberg, Rosie Sullivan, Karen Vance, Katelyn Wilson, Jacqueline Wheeler, and many others.

Many thanks to the nearly 100 students who participated in some form of experimentation related to this work. The testimonials chosen offered the broadest cross-section of experience and were edited for clarity and succinctness.

# Acknowledgments

My deepest gratitude to my main four contributors on this book: Chris Hopwood, Jason Moser, Jonathon Novello, and Marika Reisberg. Their guidance was invaluable. They gave freely of their time and expertise.

To two experts in their field who also contributed generously: Dr. Mark Seton, whose work on actors' wellbeing should become part of standard practices in acting programs; and Dr. Thalia Goldstein, who understands the importance of studying the psychology of actors.

To the graduate and undergraduate students so willing to be part of the exploration process: what they and I discovered was so exciting. I thank them for their trust.

To the many interviewed for the book who shared their experiences related to roadblocks.

The Fulbright Foundation for allowing me to complete this book in Greece. This includes the Greek office staff, especially Nicholas Tourides as well as Martin Kreeb and Katia Savrami at the University of Patras.

The College of Arts and Letters at Michigan State University for funding to complete the project.

For my colleagues at Michigan State University for their support on the book. To my wonderful friends for reading early drafts and offering notes: Barry Delaney and Lisa Herbold.

To the people who transcribed interviews and class sessions: Greg Hunter, Matt Greenbaum, Todd Neal, and Sherry Stevens.

To Carolyn Conover for her keen eye in editing.

# Preface
Roadblocks: The Self-Imposed Barriers Actors Place
on Their Work

Why do actors keep making the same choices each time they perform, even though they are playing a different character? Why do actors put limitations on their work that ultimately diminish their marketability? How can actors remain personally safe in emotionally charged scene work? How can actors identify the roadblocks that are holding them back from freedom in their work?

This book examines these and many other questions related to the self-imposed barriers actors place on their work. Roadblocks often limit and constrain actors from accessing the emotional availability so readily required for this unique craft. This book offers a systematic approach to achieving peak performance in order to defeat the self-doubt that hinders so many actors. Its aim is to assist actors in finding a previously untapped freedom in their work, a freedom that embraces stakes, vulnerability, and a lack of self-consciousness. Equally, the book offers guidance for educators and directors to compassionately assist actors toward that freedom. The book commingles psychology and acting theory in a unique way that targets the challenges that actors face daily.

The book focuses on the identification of current acting roadblocks that actors are unable to overcome and that educators are underprepared to address. It uses standardized assessments and practical exercises to assist in pinpointing possible causes for stagnancy or limitations within the actor's craft and offers realistic strategies to assist actors in achieving their fullest potential. This self-help book for actors contains strategies for identifying common emotion-based issues that performers often face. The book also features numerous tactics to guide performers to achieve flexibility, bravery, and confidence in their work, particularly in their ability to portray multiple characters that challenge their self-imposed limitations. While the book embraces an "inside out" approach to acting (where an actor begins with the identification of self in relation to the role and then emulates a character's complex psyche), the concepts discussed here are easily transferable to any approach to acting. No matter the methodology, an actor's self-imposed interior roadblocks can impede their exterior approach to performance.

This book was written under the guidance of four diverse psychology experts. (Their credentials are profiled later in the book.) They comment on the book's usefulness:

Marika Reisberg writes:

> I put a value on knowing yourself before you can become a better actor. This book is invaluable to that end. Supporting acting teachers to become healthier, more supportive coaches is imperative. There are also incredible benefits to putting value on vulnerability in acting and having a clear framework from which to teach and explore. This book holds good, ethical boundaries, which are crossed every day in theater. While there is a code of ethics for therapists, there remains none in the teaching of acting. This book begins that conversation.

Dr. Jason Moser addresses the need to examine and overcome roadblocks by noting, "Examining and being aware of one's professional impasses allows for the possibility of change and growth. It is important to first identify these challenges, and then attempt to develop strategies for new learning to take place that will ultimately help the individual achieve his or her goals."

Jonathon Novello recognizes that acting is a unique occupation, stating, "Acting requires a unique mental and cognizant awareness unlike any other profession. This need for introspection and examination of the self is necessary to improve. Acting forces introspection and requires tools to assist with this unique introspection process."

Dr. Chris Hopwood shares this comment on the book's demystification of the acting and coaching process:

> Being an actor who can identify roadblocks is an incredibly brave thing to do because you are willing to expose yourself emotionally in ways that almost nobody else does and then seek feedback. Most people have issues acknowledging what their difficulties are, receiving feedback, and then incorporating or reflecting on that criticism. In more standard jobs, you get feedback from bosses, but it's never so emotionally salient and personal as it is with acting. For an actor, part of the process is looking for that feedback, and if you can't take feedback from your director, then you can't really do the job. This book unpacks a mysterious process and allows actors to create a way for safe self-reflection and acting teachers to offer healthy feedback.

# Introduction: Roadblocks and Bridges

I argued with myself regarding the title of this book. Should it be called *Roadblocks in Acting* or *The Bridge to Acting*? The first title had a negative connotation, and while it is what much of the book is about (impediments to good acting), it seemed to leave an actor stranded and to offer no solution. The second title seemed misleading, offering a surreptitious key to becoming a famous actor. Despite the negative connotation, I decided on *Roadblocks in Acting*. I believe the title works because the book's main goal is to assist actors (as well as their teachers, coaches, and directors) in identifying, addressing, and overcoming self-imposed barriers to holistic embodied acting either on stage or on camera. So, with the title dilemma settled, let us examine the origin of the concept of "roadblocks."

I first had the idea for writing this book when I was working with some extremely talented actors in a musical theater course. They all had the knowledge, the capacity, and the skills to succeed in each assignment, but something prevented a few of them from finding freedom in their work. It was an interesting quandary that kept surfacing each time those specific students shared what they were rehearsing. Since I had been coaching them for a few years, I had a very strong understanding of their work ethic and their strengths and weaknesses as actors. They knew what their work should be. They knew what they wanted to do. They had created clear goals for their assignments. They had rehearsed, but when they presented their work, they were simply unable to produce the desired results. They were savvy enough to understand their personal limitations were holding back their acting, yet they lacked the knowledge of how to unlock or share the performances they knew they were capable of. I, too, was stymied over how best to assist them in getting the work they wanted to share out of them.

When coaching these students, I continued using the following analogy: you see what you want your work to be over there in the distance. You know what it should be. But it remains over there. There is a roadblock between you with the work you are currently sharing and the work you know you are capable of. I assisted you to get to this point. I will be waiting over there on the other side whenever you are ready to make that leap. But I have tried everything I know. It is up to you to decide when and how to build this bridge to the work you know you can do, but you are going to have to do that yourself. I'll help you with the materials and the plans, but you are going to have to make the decisions and set the schedule. You are going to have to decide when and how to build that bridge.

While the coaching contained mixed metaphors—roadblocks and bridges (both of those terms remain)—the actors and I understood what was happening to a certain point. As evidenced by the above example, it's clear that there was some sort of barricade affecting the actors. The students were unable to share their work openly and freely owing to something either internal, akin to self-sabotage, or external, perhaps in relation to environment, instructor, or peers. They recognized a roadblock—an emotionally triggered hindrance that limited freedom within their work. For our purposes then—and the book's purpose— a roadblock is not skills-based, like a deficiency in singing or dancing where an actor may simply need training to address an impediment to success. A roadblock is also not a physical limitation in a physical approach to acting where an actor lacks the requisite endurance or stamina to fully invest in the work. Rather, when the mind impedes the work by telling the actor they'll never be as talented as the other singers and dancers in class, or when an actor's physical insecurities hinder their commitment to a movement-based approach to acting, we recognize that roadblocks may affect nearly all methodologies to actor training.

What also became clear to me upon repetition of this pattern was that the teacher (me) was unable to assist the students in building a bridge to vulnerability, freedom, and confidence. It was then I realized my personal limitations as educator—a lack of knowledge related to the next level of coaching. I immediately contacted some specialists to assist.

This work demanded more than standard pedagogical or classroom management assistance. Teaching acting is a unique profession related to teacher-guided self-exploration by the actor, and I felt the territory I was headed into was dicey to say the least. So, I worked with four psychology experts for two years to assist in offering strategies to help actors find freedom in their work. They granted interviews, guided my research, observed classes, worked with students, and debated within the group the best strategies to assist actors in overcoming these self-imposed roadblocks.

I worked closely with Dr. Chris Hopwood on an earlier book called *Inner Monologue in Acting*, and we had collaborated with each other on various projects, including offering his graduate students theatrical strategies to augment their clinical work and visiting my classes to help actors "diagnose" characters. Dr. Hopwood is an associate professor of clinical psychology at Michigan State University. He teaches graduate personality assessment and supervises student assessment and psychotherapy in the clinical psychology program. His lab focuses on personality assessment, interpersonal processes, and psychotherapy.

Dr. Jason Moser began his undergraduate career as a theater major with plans of becoming an actor, before making the natural leap to psychology. I write "natural leap" because to me, acting and psychology are inextricably linked, since an actor spends most of his/her (used interchangeably from this point in the book) time analyzing the behavior of her character. Moser is as an associate professor of psychology at Michigan State University and is interested in how different ways of thinking impact cognitive and emotional processes. For example, he studies how, on the one hand, negative ways of thinking affect reactions to mistakes and attention, while, on the other hand, the same negative thinking might affect one's ability to manage emotions. Moser utilizes a multimethod approach to tackling these issues, drawing from clinical, cognitive, and social psychology, psychophysiology, and neuroscience.

I first met Jonathon Novello when he agreed to consult on a production of Tracy Letts' *Bug* I was directing. Jon is a licensed clinical social worker with the State of Michigan. Jon's areas of practice include working with adults and children dealing with depression, anxiety, addiction, grief and loss, physical illness and debilitation, and major life transitions such as divorce. His approach is eclectic, drawing from a wide range of theoretical techniques, including cognitive, behavioral, and family systems models. However, underneath his approach lies a basic set of principles that speaks to how we all operate psychologically—that all of us have our own answers, but that sometimes our understanding and beliefs of the past or the future get in the way of seeing those answers.

Marika Reisberg approaches her work from a more physical place. She is a licensed professional counselor in Colorado and performer who holds a BFA in Acting and an MA in Somatic Counseling Psychology: Dance/Movement Therapy. She has taught at Naropa University, has had extensive training in dialectical behavioral therapy (DBT) and mindfulness, and has run intensive outpatient programs in behavioral health in hospital settings. By combining her degrees in acting and psychology, she developed a series of workshops and classes to support performers and artists in sustaining creativity and working toward an embodied self.

You can more clearly understand the differences between these respected professionals by their answers to a question I posed to them at a group meeting: "How would you assist an actor in overcoming fears of physical and emotional intimacy within a scene?"

**Hopwood:** From a clinical perspective, if the actor was a patient, we would do a lot of assessment in the beginning—get questionnaire data, have observers watch the sessions, get informants or people from their lives to report on them. Sometimes we use smartphones when they go out, and every time they have an interaction with somebody, they record what the other person was like, what they were like, and how they felt, so we get lots of different data. We have them tell stories to standardized pictures, and every time we collect our data, we sort of filter that through the question, "What about these data findings helps me understand something about your issue?"

**Moser:** I guess the first thing I'd want to know is what it is about physical and emotional intimacy that's scaring them. I try to identify what the core fear is—so, "What is it really about these things that bothers you?"—and ask them for lots of examples, and then set up scenarios where they can get a chance to see, essentially, those fears realized. They have this idea in their heads of what it means to be emotionally and physically intimate. Really challenging the idea because there's something there that makes it seem scary to them, and I want to know what that is and hope to know that, over time, by testing out that this is your fear.

**Novello:** I would be initially curious as to what may have led to that fear. I'd wonder if there's something in there. I wonder what generated it. And I might spend a little time with their narrative. I might have them talk and offer some more detail about that past issue. Like the fear itself, and as they're saying things, I keep listening and being curious. Exploring where they are emotionally.

**Reisberg:** I would separate emotional intimacy and physical intimacy and look at them separately because to keep them together can be overwhelming. I would say, "Which is more prevalent for you in this moment?" I would ask them questions about their definition of physical intimacy: "How are they defining or describing it?"; "What does it feel like in their bodies?"; "Do they ever feel like they have had physical intimacy?" And similarly to emotional intimacy, "What does that mean?" I think from an embodied perspective, even when we are talking about physical intimacy or emotional intimacy, paying attention to what's happening in your body is important. Look for physical clues as a launching place for further embodied exploration.

As you can glean, they each have a unique perspective on the issue, and while there were certainly areas of overlap, the interesting part of working on this book has been the divergent tactics they could offer. Throughout the book, their guidance has assisted in creating strategies that can help actors to overcome those self-imposed roadblocks and create a bridge to more freedom in their acting. The book presents the consultants' expertise as a way to offer actors a psychologically based self-help book to assist them in realizing their full, unlimited potential.

## A Note to Actors

In order to successfully tackle any role, an actor must be adept, skilled, and vulnerable. Let us examine each of those adjectives related to the word "actor."

**Adept:** An actor's adeptness can be defined as your ability to immediately receive stimuli from scene partners while juggling the given circumstances of the script and aligning with the guidance of the director.

**Skilled:** An actor's skills extend to your ability to perform your duties related to adeptness and vulnerability without delay to the production.

**Vulnerable:** An actor's vulnerability extends to your compassionate understanding of a character in combination with an empathetic ability to explore emotional territory required by the script.

While certainly there are more qualities that define an actor, this book explores these three in various combinations. The ultimate goal is to assist an actor in demonstrating these three qualities when approaching any role. These values, when not fully employed by the actor, can stall your work to a point where you seem to be:

"Playing the same choices over and over."
"Afraid to commit emotionally."
"Not in the moment."

These comments and others usually point to a roadblock within the actor's work.

*Actor and Self*

While actors don't like to admit it, sometimes emotional limitations in your personal lives impede your work as actors. The mining of emotional territory, the need for deep introspection, and the necessity to think like the character requires a nearly impossible availability and flexibility for any person. Dr. Chris Hopwood notes, "Actors must be free, be present, and be curious." And while, as an actor, you would probably all agree with Dr. Hopwood's assessment, too often actors limit freedom and curiosity through design, by making characters as similarly developed as you are personally. Rather than fully embracing the given circumstances, creating a unique character, and pushing yourself to unexpected territory, you create characters that have the same ethics, intelligence, and sense of humor as you do because that is what you know. For a myriad of reasons that this book will explore, you can limit your work.

While always starting with the self as the basis for any character, for some, the work stops there. If asked to portray a situation in a script that you fear or that challenges you, you might resist and impose personal barriers because the situation the character is experiencing also brings up those same feelings in your personal self— feelings you might wish to avoid. The line here is blurry. What are your limitations as an actor, and how are they impacted by your personal restrictions? This book acknowledges this dangerous conundrum and seeks to assist the actor in remaining focused on the craft despite the obvious crossover.

At various stages in life, both actors and human beings are capable of handling or processing only what they allow. Often actors find that, when returning to a similar scene or a role that challenged them in the past, they can more easily master the work in their second attempt because of various explanations, including maturity, familiarity, and life experience. However, your wish to be adept, skilled, and vulnerable craftsmen does not permit for such time and distance. Our goal is to be able to tackle such territory immediately, which does not allow for roadblocks.

Maintaining a healthy synergy between self and actor requires a commitment to both physical and emotional health. It requires constant and honest examination and introspection. It also requires honesty related to what you may discover. Moser concurs, "I think openness, acceptance, and transparency are key. These are the foundations for working effectively in relation to self and actor."

### Acting Is Not Therapy

This book may be classified as a self-help book for actors because the goal is to expand the actor's range through a deeper understanding of self. Implicit in this book is the belief that acting is psychologically based and dependent upon the synthesis of the given circumstances of the script in conjunction with the actor's unfettered imagination. No one methodology will work for all actors. You may eschew this type of approach and respond more readily to skills-based or physical actor training. You may believe that this approach is merely a way of working within an American-based approach that avoids the recognized approaches of actor training in your region. The myriad approaches to acting across the globe suggests only one thing: there is no standard method for teaching all actors. This book springs from the psychologically based work of Stanislavski and filters it through various, mostly American, acting methodologists who acknowledge the actor's need for identification and reasonable understanding of the issues or emotions within a script in order to enact them realistically. Within that paradigm, it is accepted that the actor must be the arbiter when exploring that emotion or the transference of a past situation to decide when it can be used with ease and without causing personal distress. Use only the emotions you are willing to explore, emotions that have been given healthy distance, as fodder for such examination, and use all with great caution. Some issues are too current or deeply ingrained to be dealt with, and actors must recognize that. Time and emotional distance are sometimes necessary for such self-reflective work. I am not implying using affective memory (thinking of personal past situations) when performing. I use the idea more aligned with Uta Hagen's work with transference (using the essence of past experiences to substitute and help the actor understand the given circumstances of the script). Even with transferences, some relationships, memories, and experiences are not yet ready for deeper examination.

Throughout the book, the issues that impede actors may be intimately linked to emotional terrain that you should not examine at the current time. And despite the fact that the book espouses numerous proven psychological and therapeutic theories and practices, these are for actors to embrace only when you are fully able. Deciding when to tackle these roadblocks must be carried out with personal care and consideration.

Conversely, when an actor's personal catharsis becomes more important than their character's, the balance of acting has shifted from a healthy examination of personal, emotional availability to the indulgent and self-involved actor placating some non-acting need. The cliché of the tortured artist is something that can be erased through honest reflection and realistic goals. There is a difficult balance between indulgence and necessary emotional capacity, so the areas must be traversed with sensitivity.

Reisberg remembers all too well the unique and emotionally challenging perspective of the actor: "I was trained to be a really skilled actor, but I wasn't skilled to handle all the stuff that comes with being a performer. And how do you set it all aside and go wait tables, or go have a relationship with someone who's not in your field, or be a parent, or deal with your laundry?" Actors have a unique profession that demands unique life skills.

Every actor's path is different. And every solution to an actor's roadblock is individualized. It is up to you to responsibly and honestly accept and address the issues that may be limiting your current work. Dr. Chris Hopwood expands on this: "Beyond that, knowing yourself is really a process that is multi-final, meaning that different people probably need different paths."

You may feel that this book and its definition of acting adhere closely to realism, based on its concentration on honesty in performance. This is not solely the case. Roadblocks impede the actor no matter the style in which they are asked to play. You may recognize a roadblock when it impedes your freedom from unencumbered thought when improvising in a commedia dell'arte mask, constrains you from feeling like truly one of the ensemble in a Greek chorus, traps you in the present when performing a Shakespeare history play, or limits your expressiveness in an expressionistic play. Roadblocks appear in any style of acting and insidiously disallow your ability to commit fully to acting—no matter the style. The definition of acting in this "A Note to Actors" introductory section and the rest of the book honors honesty and authenticity in performance, which may be a foundation (albeit augmented) in most styles of acting.

### Actor and Acting Teacher

Pushing boundaries, exploring new situations in a safe environment, and raising the dramatic stakes beyond what the actor may first consider should be what acting class is about, right? Certainly. But, again, the actor must be the arbiter. While you as a student in class or an actor in rehearsal should be willing to navigate all of the emotional requirements within the script, you must also develop a strategic plan with your acting teacher or director. Honest two-way discussions, frank exploration, and realistic goals are the keys to finding freedom within your work.

Actors should also read the similarly named section for acting teachers in "A Note to Acting Teachers" on p. 10. I would suggest actors also read all the information for educators throughout the book, as it will offer a chance for you to understand boundaries and ethical issues while also allowing you to become a better advocate for the work you want to do. Too often we blindly trust our teachers and directors, and that can lead to even more roadblocks. Trust is earned. Your acting teacher may enter into assisting you with your road-block only at your invitation. That invitation may also be retracted at your request if you feel overwhelmed or uncomfortable. I once had an acting teacher who made us strip off a different piece of clothing each time we "revealed" personal information about our past. I have worked with directors who asked the cast to expose their darkest secrets in order to bond and create a "safe" environment. Too often actors are willing to cross these ethical boundaries because you want to impress your director, or you don't want to ruin the ensemble, or because you think this is the way to get to honesty in acting. An actor must be willing to commit fully as participant while also advocating for a safe environment.

Being an adept, vulnerable, and skilled actor requires an understanding of your chosen profession as a conduit for human emotion. Your job is to "live" in highly emotional situations that require an acute understanding of the self. It is also necessary to have a strong focus on the process with professional rather than therapeutic goals. And finally, it is key to enter into explorative development in the classroom or rehearsal with an awareness of the process. These guidelines are necessary for your work as actor in order to begin eradicating roadblocks.

## A Note to Acting Teachers

In order to be successful in the classroom, an acting teacher must be adept, skilled, and vulnerable. Let us examine each of those adjectives related to the word "teacher."

**Adept:** A teacher's adeptness can be defined as your ability to immediately respond to work with precise notes as well as offering big-picture linkages that can assist students in seeing patterns in their work.

**Skilled:** A teacher's skills extend to your ability to assist various actors with various issues in various ways, adapting to and recognizing actor needs and supplying them with guidance and assistance depending on the learning style of the actor.

**Vulnerable:** A teacher's vulnerability relates to the empathetic understanding of the challenges that actors may face, as well as compassion for the difficulty of their work.

While certainly there are more qualities that define a teacher, these three, in various combinations, are what this book explores. The ultimate goal is to assist an educator to demonstrate these three qualities when assisting an actor with roadblocks. These values, when not employed strategically, can leave the educator frustrated, saying things like:

"She'll get there on her own."
"They're too young to get it."
"I just don't know how to reach him."

These comments and others usually point to a need for more strategies to assist actors with their personal roadblocks.

## Teacher and Self

The primary goal of an acting teacher is to help actors in creating honest and vulnerable work. Some of our work as teachers includes guiding students to an exploration of territory that is emotionally challenging, sexually provocative, or politically charged. An acting teacher must maintain professional distance while also encouraging a student to risk, commit, and explore work that scares or confuses them.

The acting studio must be a safe space that remains protected, open, and free of judgment. I think we all, as acting teachers, wish that to be true, but that sort of ensemble-based utopia can sometimes be very difficult to build. Unexpected group dynamics, unobserved peer-to-peer interactions, contradictory notes from the instructor, and many other variables impact the studio as a safe space. The last description of the acting studio as a place free from judgment is particularly challenging, as feedback, no matter how innocent and constructive in its intent, can always be perceived as critique. Marika Reisberg expands on the notion of a safe environment: "I don't know if you've experienced going into a rehearsal space and the director saying, 'this is a safe space.' But no one's talking about what safety is, who's responsible for it, who's holding it, who's maintaining it. So that, to me, is a disservice to performers."

To me, the hardest part about being an acting teacher is the subjectivity of it all. My personal aesthetic for what is honest seems to rule the feedback and creates similarly minded/brainwashed actors who value my definition of honesty. What seems "real" to me now seems "real" to them. That is a great responsibility, and too often teachers lose sight of that influence. This reminder of subjectivity also impacts your work with roadblocks. Assisting the student in achieving the work they are capable of should be evaluated by the student whenever possible.

I also find it difficult to remember not to direct the actors when in the classroom. In these studios, my goal is to help students unlock and achieve their potential and I sometimes find myself interrupting that process by acting as director in the classroom. I forget the classroom distinction because I see an actor so close to understanding a concept, and I know it will be easier if I just tell them how to get there. The result is lazy teaching and a lesson that will not be retained because the student will merely parrot back my choices rather than making them for themselves. So, even when I have recognized an actor's roadblock in class, I cannot simply tell them what to do to overcome it. I must guide and assist them in their own discovery process.

## Acting Teachers Are Not Therapists

Just as acting is not therapy, teaching acting does not turn an acting teacher into a therapist. The "American" method of harnessing and understanding emotion in order to enact it within the given circumstances of the script may seem like an invitation to insinuate yourself into the emotional, interior life of the student. It is not. Despite the personal problems students may share with you, the openness with which they may discuss the themes of a controversial play, or the information you may have gleaned from a discussion on building a sexually driven character, your purview should remain focused on how to assist them in their onstage lives. You must assist in helping the actor explore the territory they deem safe and necessary. Knowing when to allow students to stop that exploration is imperative to the process. While the teacher is there to assist, the actor sets the parameters for healthy exploration of roadblocks.

Many acting teachers do not subscribe to this emotion-based approach to acting and find that their entrance into teaching acting is a more skills-based method. Some may approach teaching acting from a physical point of view. As mentioned in the "A Note to Actors" section, when these approaches are hindered by the actor's inner thoughts manifesting themselves in insecurity or self-imposed limitations, this book can assist in freeing the actor. Whatever the methodology, it should be clear that when an actors' reticence is related to their own barriers, a roadblock is at play.

The clichés of the acting teacher as guru, confessor, or therapist can be shattered by creating channels of communication that direct information related to their offstage life to people better equipped to handle such affairs. Working with some roadblocks can get overly personal, and even if the student gives permission, you as teacher must have the wherewithal to know when you are in over your head. In these moments, it is always best to recommend that trained professionals would better serve the student to address their personal issues. When that is completed, you can be there to assist in helping the student to become a better actor. The territory of this book should not give license to acting teachers to overstep student–teacher relationships.

### Actor and Acting Teacher

Similar to the two stories I shared in the "A Note to Actors" section, Reisberg recalls issues she has observed in acting classes in the past:

> Having been to acting school, a lot of the time we were given these assignments where you really had to "filet" yourself emotionally and be really vulnerable in front of people that you didn't know. I mean you kind of knew your classmates in acting, but you didn't necessarily have a solid foundation of knowing these people—what their backgrounds were, etcetera. Or you had teachers who were asking you to be incredibly vulnerable while some of the techniques that they chose to use were pretty detrimental and pretty trauma inducing. And at the end of the class, you were then told, "Great! See you next week!" And, I just remember students walking out, disassociating, and asking each other, "What was that?" or "How did that just happen?" or by experiencing vicarious trauma watching people you really care about doing monologues or scenes with these emotional triggers happening and not knowing what to do or how to help them. So, how, as a young actor, do you differentiate between what's mine, what's theirs, what's the character's? And so, over the years, I've talked to a lot of performers, educators, and therapists about how to develop a curriculum to support performers so they have a foundation of safety and trust that they can take with them wherever they go.

I wish I could report that these types of stories are generational and the new breed of acting teachers understands those boundaries. I am not certain that is the case. As Reisberg wrote in the overview, there are codes of ethics in various occupations, and as we continue to work so closely with actors, it is important to be reminded of the ethical questions that the coaching in the above story raises.

Either as student or as teacher, you may have been part of a situation where an emotional breakthrough occurred and then you wondered what might remain when the scene was over. An emotionally naked and vulnerable actor who has summoned up high-stakes emotions, probably for the first time, is left "fileted" as class ends and real life returns. For some, that moment can be the first time they felt that electricity related to the accessing of emotion, and they are primed and eager for more experimentation. But for others, those new emotions displayed in front of peers or strangers deserve extra coaching, decompression, and assimilation to assist with these freshly accessed feelings.

I write in such a cautionary manner because early on in this exploration I went too far with a student who seemed desperate to address his roadblock to access vulnerability. I could see the actor on the precipice of a breakthrough, so I coached aggressively and tirelessly. When scant progress was made and class was over, the actor was left despondent, defeated, and devastated. This feeing impacted him quite deeply for the next few weeks both in class and beyond. I lacked the skills to pick up the pieces of what I had wrought. Weeks later, the student was able to achieve the work he wanted to, but the earlier day of coaching kept me hyper-aware in future instruction to be more sensitive to the signs I had ignored based on the student's eagerness. For while an actor may indicate he is willing to work on certain issues, sometimes he might not be emotionally ready. As educator, I should have responded to unspoken signals from the student that the coaching might have been too much—such as breath, mounting frustration, and tenseness in performance—and ended the exploration much earlier than I did. I have since learned sharper skills and have been more vigilant about such boundary-crossings and can report no other such complications in later roadblock work. Throughout the book, you will read about emotional limits and boundaries. These are included to assist you to avoid a similar situation.

As noted by my example, the role of acting teacher is a great responsibility. Eager and open students look to you for guidance into deeply emotional territory. It is easy to misuse that influence. The difficult balancing act related to the subject of this book should not be used to allow the teacher to play any role other than that of teaching acting.

# 1    A Roadblock

In the following transcript, playwright and director Dr. Ann Folino White is interviewed on her experience working on an original play called *The Lady Victory*. The show is about a Catholic school for young, unwed mothers and is adapted from a book of poems by Jane Vincent Taylor. As playwright and director, Dr. Folino White found a student actor incapable of producing the needed emotional state for the show. In the scene, the actor was asked to simulate early signs of labor. In this example of how an actor's roadblock in action can affect more than just herself, Dr. Folino White talks about her frustration with the actor, her strategies to assist the actor, and her eventual decision to rewrite the scene for a different actor who was capable of portraying the high stakes necessary.

Also interviewed is the actor Melissa Mercieca, who is asked to examine her experience and how her personal roadblocks perplexed her ability to offer what was needed in the scene. The interview includes strategies related to how the actor eventually overcame her personal acting impediment and found freedom in her later work. Present in these interviews is graduate researcher Sarah Goeke, who also appeared in the production.

**Roznowski:** So, tell us about working on *The Lady Victory*, specifically this intense scene with Melissa Mercieca.

**Folino White:** The scene had originally been written so that the character played by Melissa would go into labor, and the reason that it had been written as [that character] going into labor was due to the fact that the character was a leader, a model of control. And, as the playwright, I felt as if that character losing control and showing great vulnerability and fear was poetic. Melissa showed the qualities of leadership in her audition and throughout the rehearsals very easily—that comes very easy to her, taking control of a room and being the center of the attention. What became apparent was that the actor was very uncomfortable with being physically vulnerable. This scene required imitating the pain and fear that go along with going into labor; particularly for the first time, when a woman actually hasn't any sense of what it is, until it's occurring.

**Roznowski:** What were some of the things you noticed?

**Folino White:** One thing that tends to trip young women actors specifically is not being beautiful on stage. So, there's a self-consciousness that goes into the performance where they become aware of how they look. So, that is what I mean by "physically vulnerable." There was no physical danger in the process, but rather the pain of labor that I wanted her to mimic that required a freeness of the body and a freeness to look foolish and ugly and physically unsure in a way that a lot of actors in my experience translate into, "People are going to see me and judge my appearance or think that I am ugly." What I try to express to actors is that if you are open, imaginative, free, and committed on the stage—no matter what it is that you look like—you will become beautiful to the audience because they're emotionally connected to you, and the appearance falls to a secondary position in terms of the audience connection to the character.

**Roznowski:** What tactics did you try to assist the actor?

**Folino White:** Melissa had watched labor videos. I had talked to her about my experience of labor and where it is located and sort of how "shame" leaves you because there are so many people in a room and you are exposed in all sorts of ways. And how your primary concern is for your safety and the physical safety of the child. And fear and hope of the unknown take hold, as does the pain. Melissa also spoke with another female faculty member who had gone through the childbirth process three times and under very different circumstances than mine. So, that was part of the preparatory process. And we talked about how it's very difficult for a person who's never been through it to know what it's like and the fear associated with going through something for the first time. And, then, I realized the actor was unable to produce both the physical manifestations of that pain as well as the related emotional content of the fear and the sorrow of losing the child or knowing that the child would be taken from her. The actor repeatedly said the words, "I know I can do it, I just need to go work on it on my own." I responded repeatedly with, "No, you must be able to work in front of me and in front of an audience." And so we, all of the women [in the cast] were working on this scene, we laid down, including me, on the floor as a group and just screamed as an exercise in effort of "collectivity" so that the actor wasn't left alone to do it herself on the stage.

**Goeke:** You were really on her side, in her process, not demanding anything, and you would say, "It hasn't gotten any better—what do you feel?" She would say things like, "I don't know." She was confused in the moment, too. She was young and confused. I was looking at Melissa and feeling so bad because she just did not know what to do. It was not coming from a place of laziness or anything. And then it became you seeing that she needs a script for this part. And that's when you said, "You feel it here." "You do it there." "This is what happens." "Then this happens on this line." So she didn't have to make any choices or feel vulnerable that way.

**Folino White:** I created a physical script because the actor expressed that she didn't have the tools to do it herself. She would say, "I'm having trouble." "I'm stuck again." "I think I almost really got there."

**Goeke:** I do remember that during the process no one was ever mad at her—because the actor did her work.

**Folino White:** There was never that sort of negative feedback because it was such a difficult scene, and I didn't think that sort of coaching would motivate the actor. Sometimes that [negative feedback] really motivates the actor, and it's a really good tactic, but with this particular actor, I think it would have shut her down further.

**Roznowski:** What was the moment when you made the decision to change the play related to the actor's roadblock?

**Folino White:** I said, "This is the change that I'm thinking of making" and that I was going to switch who was going into labor in terms of the character and restructure parts of the play to allow that to be a logical thing to happen because the other actor in the scene was more advanced in her education and also an actor who, while not capable of being leader, was incredibly comfortable with deep vulnerability—both physical and emotional; that was really that actor's strength.

**Goeke:** My perception was that it was done without any malice. Because in situations like that, I've seen directors hold it against the actor, [and the director] can be really angry or chiding or condescending. This wasn't condescending; it was a frank and thorough explanation. It's a skill set. It was like that person knows how to carve wood and this person doesn't, and so I'm going to have that person make the chair. It was very straightforward.

**Roznowski:** How do you think Melissa responded? And how did it affect the next rehearsals, the run of show, and the ensemble?

**Folino White:** She responded with terrible grace. I'm not privy to how she responded outside of my presence and that could have been very different because I'm not only her director; I'm her teacher. And she was going to be stuck with me for three years. So, I can't respond to that—I know that she was upset and we talked about how I thought she was embarrassed. Because no matter what I did, it was singling her out as incapable of doing something. And so, I think that what I achieved in the discussion with that entire group was mitigating and minimizing her embarrassment by being honest: "If we had time, it might be possible, but we're out of time," and by suggesting that it wasn't a matter of innate talent, because I don't believe in that, but that it had to do with skill development. And that the other actor had more time and training than Melissa did. And Melissa eventually said, "I think the play's better now because it allows [this other character] to have her moment in the sun." So, the actor felt as though she contributed in a way; her failing improved the play because the change in the script allowed for another character to have a very poetic and beautiful moment. So, I think she felt like she contributed.

Melissa Mercieca, the actor discussed in the above transcript, was also interviewed for the book. It must be noted that she and Dr. Folino White currently have an outstandingly healthy and respectful relationship. Following *The Lady Victory*, they have worked together twice and both recognize that the actor has gained skills, confidence, and resiliency since this initial issue.

**Mercieca:** I had been involved in the workshop production, so I knew the play.

**Roznowski:** And when you read the script and you saw what you were going to have to go through—what did you feel?

**Mercieca:** I was really nervous.

**Roznowski:** Why?

**Mercieca:** I was extremely nervous because I wanted to prove that I could do it.

**Roznowski:** To whom?

**Mercieca:** Everybody. And Ann. Anyway, so I was very, very nervous and didn't expect the role at all—I expected to be put back in the ensemble somewhere. So, it caught me really off guard that she thought that I could do it. So, the first thing that I did was set up a meeting with her to talk about what she expected from the role, and she said, "Just go for it and don't hold anything back," because sometimes in the workshop I would be nervous reading for roles and wouldn't completely go all the way and hold back—which is the issue that I had a lot, you know. So, reading it over that winter break and taking notes and stuff like that, I was so convinced that I was just going to do it, and then I found at rehearsals I couldn't let go. The thing that had me most nervous is that I had never been in that situation. I think that I was trying to inflict the physical pain onto myself and figure out what it felt like. I had a meeting with another professor about her labor experiences because she had had some terrible labor experiences to try and get a sense of what it felt like, and I think physically what I was doing was trying to clench all of the muscles in my body to make it painful. And it just ...

**Roznowski:** It just clenched you up as an actor?

**Mercieca:** Yes.

**Roznowski:** So, you are in rehearsal, you start working on it. You're about to do that scene for the first time. What did you feel?

**Mercieca:** I remember sitting in the read-through thinking, "Okay, it's coming ... okay, it's coming ... you're just going to do it ... you're just going to read the scene and you're going to be fine," and then I just read it. Ann said, "I need more." And I thought, "You're just going to do it with all the sounds of labor and it's going to be fine." And, I couldn't convince myself that it wasn't going to be embarrassing.

**Roznowski:** Embarrassing for you in front of your peers?

**Mercieca:** Yeah, me having this experience was going to make me look like an idiot, and I was going to be terrible. I think I was afraid of looking stupid and foolish.

**Roznowski:** So, then, as it went along, when did it become a big problem?

**Mercieca:** I would do the scene, and I couldn't get anywhere with it, and as soon as the scene was over, I would be sobbing. And so I was trying everything I could to open myself up. I worked outside of rehearsal with other actors where they literally held me down to the ground while I was screaming, but I couldn't get myself anywhere emotionally.

**Roznowski:** Even with all your friends?

**Mercieca:** Yeah, and I think that I was trying too hard to cry because I thought that mattered. I didn't want it to be bad, and I was so afraid that letting go and just doing it would make it terrible.

**Roznowski:** Whereas you knew at the same time that you weren't fulfilling what the role needed?

**Mercieca:** So Ann said, "I think I'm going to rewrite the scene." And that completely devastated me. Because I knew that I could do it, and I remember that every break that we took in rehearsal, I'd stop and run away to the bathroom. I was so petrified. And then we talked about it, and then she rewrote the scene, and I read the rewrite and I liked it better. So, then the scene got better. I think I had two more rehearsals with me doing [the old version] after the rewrite, and Ann said that those were better. I kept getting better after that because it felt like the pressure was off; I liked the rewrite, and I wasn't so worried about ruining the play anymore. So, then, she was so wonderful. She made me part of the decision; she made me feel like I was part of the decision to do the alternate ending.

**Roznowski:** You keep saying things about "looking foolish." What would make you look foolish? What's the most foolish thing that could happen?

**Mercieca:** Nothing could have happened. I don't know why I was so worried about it. I understand why I was uncomfortable with the actual act of what was happening—the screaming and that kind of thing. The idea of having to stand on stage and scream in agony makes me uncomfortable because it makes me uncomfortable to watch other people do it.

**Roznowski:** Do you know why?

**Mercieca:** Um ... I don't know why.

**Roznowski:** What allowed you to find freedom in your current work?

**Mercieca:** I think I got out of my own way. I also think improv has helped. Because that—really for the first time—taught me if you screw up and you're in an improv show, you can't think about it for the rest of the day or the rest of the show, because there are people watching you and you're making up everything on the spot; if you're worried about something that you messed up in the first two minutes, thirty minutes later, when you're still improvising, no one cares—it's no big deal. No one cares that you've screwed up.

**Roznowski:** So, it seems like that's the through-line here: "I didn't want to look foolish"; "I didn't want people to judge me"; "I want to keep myself safe."

**Mercieca:** Exactly. Yeah, but then it's like watching my friends make bold choices in acting class, and even if the choice that they made didn't work, the fact that they made the choice is what I remember—not the fact that the choice didn't work. So I started working on that for myself. I started setting goals. So, when we did the autodrama [covered in Chapter 6 in the book], I forced myself to be uncomfortable, and it turned out really well. I forced myself to do something very uncomfortable. And having those successes time and time again, I feel more grounded and more open as a person. And as an actor.

**Roznowski:** So any idea what prevented you from making that discovery earlier?

**Mercieca:** I think I was so obsessed with what everyone else thought about me that I didn't necessarily like myself as an actor. I didn't know that then. But learning to trust myself, and in extension others, by pushing myself in acting classes and setting goals in rehearsals has allowed me to find that freedom on stage.

It is evident that one actor's personal roadblocks can hinder an entire production. You may note the productive way in which a destructive issue was handled by both actor and director. In both Dr. Folino White's and Ms. Mercieca's interview, it is clear that great compassion was shown to the actor in relation to her roadblock. Dr. Folino White's adroit approach was respectful and supportive while also keeping the needs of the production significant. You may also note that she offered several technically based suggestions as well as physical solutions, both of which did not work for an actor consumed by a roadblock. This highlights the equal impact of internal roadblocks on external approaches to acting. In this case, the reworking of the script, as the playwright allowed for a drastic revision, related to the roadblock; such revision cannot always occur. Also, the luxury of academic theater, in most cases, is that the process has a component of education at its core, and this allowed more time for the exploration of the issue, whereas, in most professional productions, the actor is expected to be the immediate master of a multitude of skills.

The roadblock not only impeded a production but "devastated" an actor. It is evident that the student tried various strategies to address her roadblock during rehearsal, albeit unsuccessfully. At the time, Ms. Mercieca lacked the introspection, vocabulary, and experience necessary to bridge her work to take it to the place she knew it needed to be. Luckily, the actor was able to piece together a way to transform her work to a more open place, most likely incited by the disturbing events from the earlier production. By placing herself in situations like improvisation, that challenged her fear of "looking foolish," Ms. Mercieca was able to recognize the misplaced importance she put on others' reaction to her work. Additionally, after acutely observing her peers making bold choices (sometimes unsuccessfully) in their craft, she also began to take risks in her own work. Once she recognized that the importance she placed on the opinion of others held more importance than the value of her own opinion, she was essentially able to retrain herself as an actor. Although it was post performance, the respectful handling by the director and the fortitude of the actor eradicated the roadblock.

Dr. Thalia R. Goldstein, who has written on the importance of why cognitive scientists should study acting, revealed to me in an interview her insight: "I think that anything that blocks an actor from empathy—from being able to understand why someone does an action, without judgment—will be a block. So if that means figuring out a way to remove self-judgment about actions, and to remove prejudice towards others—in any form, then that's what actors have to do to fully understand characters." It is this process of removal of barriers that this book covers. Such a removal of impediments can and does occur and can lead to a richer life as an actor.

Following her reading of this chapter prior to publication, Dr. Ann Folino White wrote me a postscript that may act as a way to prepare you for the work on which you are about to embark. As teacher or actor, it is important to remind yourself of the manner in which this sort of work is handled. Dr. Folino White writes:

> It was therapeutic to read both my and Melissa's reflections. It was an incredibly difficult decision, and I still don't know if it was the right one, but I am confident that, together, Melissa and I handled it beautifully and that our expressed mutual respect for one another (and our production) was key to helping both of us improve as artists. By which I mean, it seems that how roadblocks are handled is vital to whether they are overcome, regardless of when they are overcome.

Folino White's final sentiments regarding the means rather than the end are important for both educator and actor.

Melissa Mercieca also sent a follow-up after her reading of this chapter. The questions she poses are asked by many actors experiencing roadblocks:

> It was a relief to read Ann's side of the story because I had continually asked myself, "What if I had worked harder?"; "What if I had tried harder?"; "What if I had spent more time and made fewer excuses?" All the tears, sleepless nights, and confusion were worth it. If this situation hadn't been handled with such mutual respect, trust, and love, I know my roadblock would have become [permanent], and I'm not sure if I would have been an actor for much longer.

Ms. Mercieca's final sentiment regarding leaving acting because of a roadblock makes me question how many actors have felt similar limitations in their work but were unable to address them. How many have succumbed to roadblocks?

The issue of roadblocks is not unique to the production discussed or to one way of actor training. Actors are tasked daily by directors, casting directors, playwrights, screenwriters, educators, and more to perform material that challenges them. As evidenced in the above interviews, your response to those challenges may be to limit the choices to only the safe and standard ones you normally make. This, as Dr. Jason Moser notes, allows you to act with, "Only emotions you have processed, vetted, and find acceptable." Acting choices made out of complacency are one issue, but this book examines the choices that are currently unavailable based on a self-imposed impediment. In order to open yourself to the vast array of possibilities currently lacking in your acting arsenal, you may choose to examine roadblocks.

# 2    Understanding Yourself as Actor

In this chapter and those that follow, you will examine the foundational work related to identifying roadblocks and eventually removing them, using strategies and exercises that were tested in some form by nearly 100 students in numerous undergraduate and graduate acting courses over several years. Three courses were specifically devoted to testing the theories of this book, while other courses provided a chance to workshop specific exercises and theories. The psychology experts in the book consulted on the construction of the syllabi and visited the courses to offer immediate feedback to the questions raised by the work. The testimonial that follows (like those in the rest of the book) was written by a student and submitted following their studies on roadblocks.

*I never really took the chance to self-examine and figure out what the weaknesses were in my acting abilities. I knew they existed, of course; I know that everyone has something that they are working towards, some nebulous goal just on the horizon that we are all constantly chugging towards, and I know that most people have some sort of obstacle in the way of that goal. However, I never had a word to describe the concept. I knew that I was previously aware of things that I could and could not do; sometimes acutely so. I just always thought that those things were something I had to ignore. Not because I didn't want to work on them, or I was under some misapprehension that they weren't affecting my work; I just didn't realize that these obstacles—these roadblocks—were something that we as actors would ever be encouraged to address. I always thought of them as something of an "out of sight, out of mind" type thing. I have since realized that I was very wrong. The only way to get past these roadblocks is to address them; to acknowledge the problem, tear down the wall, and progress onto the next thing.*

## Why Are You an Actor?

This simple question can confound you. Your initial answer may be, "I just am." Or "I always have been." Or "Because I can't do anything else." These answers, while perhaps personally valid, lack the core motivation as to why, out of all of the various pathways a person may take, you decided to choose the difficult job of being an actor. This odd profession, unlike any other, requires you to inhabit another and then publicly display your work for audience critique. It must be asked again, "Why are you an actor?"

While there are a myriad of answers, most can be categorized into two primal motivations. Dr. Jason Moser states, "Many become an actor because they are gregarious; they like the attention. Or they do it to lose their self—to hide. Both are trying to fill an emotional void." Moser does aver that there is more nuance to the classification and reasoning for acting. For many, the idea of narrowing down your approach to acting discussed within this chapter may feel reductionist, but the reasoning for such narrow classifications is to allow the actor a chance to more readily and handily identify your approach to the craft. It should be noted that within these controlled categorizations, you may more easily begin the work of self-identification related to roadblocks. Let us examine two possible motivations for entering this field.

For some, acting was initially a chance to become the center of attention—to be in the spotlight and thrive on recognition from others. For those people, deeply affected by the laughter and applause, notoriety was the prime impulse to begin acting. For others, their foray into acting was a chance to lose their personal inhibitions or escape daily life, an adventure to live as someone else for a while. While real life may have been unfulfilling, life on stage became a place to gain confidence or new experiences as another. Both are entirely appropriate and respectable reasons for acting.

Of course these oversimplifications can meld and morph; a shy person who goes into acting to play someone new may then become excited by the response and acceptance of others, making her a more histrionic and gregarious person. Surely each person's journey is unique, but the point is to examine the base motivation for involving yourself in the art of pretend. You should avoid the less easy answers of "Because it was fun" or "I just always loved movies," and try to fit your answer into one of the two possible categorizations Moser provides. You may call yourself a "storyteller" or avow that "you wanted to change lives though acting," but you should focus on reducing it down to its basic essence. Using one of Moser's two categories, classify the reasons you started acting in the first place.

The final part of Moser's quote is also an imperative for deeper reflection. His statement that both impulses for acting are "trying to fill an emotional void" perplexed me until I realized there was a need for this level of honesty. If I was being defensive for myself or protective of my students I was not fully embracing the level of self-reflection that I need in order to truly examine my craft. And all of us possess or have experienced emotional voids in some way in our lives. My layman's ears heard Moser's assessment as a judgment rather than the practical provocation to deeper examination of self related to art.

For actors in the preliminary roadblock courses, the question (Why are you an actor?) offered a myriad of answers that basically fell within the two areas Moser suggested. For many, the interesting result of examining their initial motivation for becoming an actor clarified their personal purpose or reinvigorated their love of acting. This outwardly benign question resulted in a multitude of outcomes. It also began the journey to identifying roadblocks.

The first exercise of this book is a chance to answer the question, "Why did you become an actor?" Did you love the feeling of being on stage because of the laughs and the applause? Did you love being the center of attention? Or were you drawn to it because you got to play someone very different from yourself? Did you thrive on becoming another? What was your main motivation? Note that I did not ask about the "emotional void." Although that lingers as part of the question, that personal information should remain so. This sort of work relies on the clear understanding and respect for the balance of what must remain with the actor and what is public knowledge.

## Exercise 2.1    Define your reason for being an actor

### What Type of Actor Are You?

Now, with a clear vision of why you became an actor, you must examine the subsequent implications. What sort of actor do those two categorizations create? While each actor's journey is unique, most actors can be sorted into two very different categories. In Rick Kemp's book, *Embodied Acting: What*

*Neuroscience Tells Us about Performance,* he classifies the two types as, "'Persona' acting versus 'transformational' acting (also known as 'personality' acting and 'character' acting.) ... My understanding of the distinction is that the 'personal' actor maintains a more or less constant personality from one role to the next, while the 'transformational' actor embodies various personalities according to the role." Similarly to Moser's two classifications, Kemp's simplification of reducing acting into two categories is used as a fundamental investigative tool through which to examine and organize your thoughts.

In very basic terms, the "personality" actor's essence remains similar from role to role, and her basic humanity is seen throughout each performance. The "character" actor "loses themselves" in the role in order to portray a variety of character types. Both are valid and viable ways to act. Kemp continues:

> The persona actor uses behavioral communicators that stay within a range that identifies his or her personality. Which remains more or less constant from one role to the next. The transformational actor displays a variety of behavioral communications according to the demands of the character. In the case of persona actors, we see the more or less constant personality responding to the fictional circumstances with reasonably predictable results—we don't expect actors like Tom Cruise and Harrison Ford to meekly surrender to adversity, for instance. We see a greater variety of behavior in actors such as Phillip Seymour Hoffman and Daniel Day-Lewis in different roles, but in neither category can we state from observation that the actors are, or are not, identifying their concepts of their "essential self" with the roles they play.

Depending on the way in which you react to the definitions, defining the type of actor you are may cause initial confusion. The personality actor may seem less versatile or the character actor might appear to be hiding behind disguises. But it must be understood that both are effective forms of acting. The difference is simply a categorization that takes a closer and more realistic look at the way in which you approach your craft. Your success in past roles may have developed into a type you play most often, or a series of scenes that may have displayed a spectrum of distinct characters seems to define your success. Whatever the reason, it is important to understand how you perceive your work. In Exercise 2.8 in this chapter, the connection to others offering their perspectives will come into play, but for now, you must decide the category into which you fall.

To assist in the ability to categorize yourself, you can explore analyzing other actors whose work you respect. Kemp's suppositions that Tom Cruise and Harrison Ford are personality actors are excellent examples. I posit that fine actors such as Tom Hanks or Julia Roberts might fall into this category as well. Similarly, the classification of Philip Seymour Hoffman and Daniel Day-Lewis as character actors may be expanded to include actors such as Johnny Depp and Meryl Streep. The ability to recognize the traits of such acting in others can make it more easily recognizable within you.

In this upcoming exercise, use the classification of "personality" or "character" to define the type of actor you are. Not what you hope to be, but what defines your current approach to acting using the classifications above. Do not allow your answer to fall into the middle or easier response: "My approach changes depending on the role." Truly examine your process and your output in order to best categorize your work. Classifications provide a way to organize your thoughts and codify your approach. Your categorization can be shared with others or remain personal information.

## Exercise 2.2   Define the type of actor you are

### What Kind of Actor Do You Want to Be?

Implicit in this book is the idea that all actors want to be embodied, creative artists who share a need to create an emotional connection with themselves and others. The adept, skilled, and vulnerable actor described earlier may not hold as much value to you. Moser notes, "You all have choices to make about what sort of actors you want to be, so I think a good place to start to examine might just be questions like: what are your goals, what are your values, what do you want to be able to do, and what do you really want to be good at?"

You may feel entirely successful in the choices you make and the actor you are. You are to be congratulated. It is important that, as an actor, you recognize your strengths. Moser continues: "We are all good at something, some things better than others. The issue is about making choices about what you want to do. What do you really want to achieve and why do you want to achieve that? Is it because you see a big value in your career to do that?" The initial questions expand to larger philosophical questions about yourself as actor and as artist and your contribution to both categories. Spend some time examining the kind of actor you are and consider the actor you want to be.

As Moser suggests, the need for such a journey related to identifying and overcoming roadblocks is not for every actor (or teacher). The melding of acting and psychology may make you uncomfortable, just as any other book related to achieving peak performance through mental focus might. Like any of the thousands of nonacting books related to overcoming the self-doubt that affects performance, you must find the concept or strategy that best connects with your goals. Similarly, this book must match your goals related to the actor you want to be. And while the book offers realism at its base, it should soon be apparent that despite the style, genre, or medium an actor is working in, the roadblock remains consistent across all. No matter the school of thought to teaching or understanding acting, there are clear ways that roadblocks may hinder the implementation.

Finding a methodology, teacher, or book that resonates with your future ambitions is of the greatest importance. This book seeks to assist actors to achieve their peak performance levels by liberating them from self-doubt and offering a systematic approach to that end. By using some examples from their own works, the consultants on the book offer some suggestions related to finding the approach that resonates best with you.

**Moser:** I'm upfront with my patients, trying to let them know what I can offer. If you're looking for insight and understanding about where your problems come from, then don't come see me. That's not what I'm about; that's not what I'm going to focus on. But if that's what you want, I'm happy to send you to Jonathon.

**Novello:** That would be me. But I imagine that crosses disciplines to acting teachers, right? Students say, "This acting teacher is really great at getting this thing from you."

**Hopwood:** I spend an awful lot of time educating clients on how to find the right person for them because nobody knows how to do that. It is a foreign concept to them. They assume you're the person for them.

Just as the consultants are aware of their boundaries in relation to their focus so should acting teachers be aware of their limitations and be honest with students regarding their approach. Similarly students should take ownership of the work they need to address in their acting and find the corresponding teacher. So, if your goals align with the focus and aim of this book, there may be a match. Matching the type of actor you want to be with the strengths of any teacher or method is essential to your success.

The use of the phrase "peak performance" has a unique definition for the actor. Usually bandied about in terms of athletes who are playing an exceptional game, where everything seems to flow, they are unstoppable, concentrated, alert, or "in the zone," peak performance does not just depend on physical strength but requires an attentive inner strength that focuses on the task at hand and transports the athletes to heights that surprise even them.

For the actor, peak performance can be described as a moment of performing with a complete lack of consciousness. By that, I mean there is absolutely no self-consciousness—you are not worried about how you look or how you sound. There is also a loss of "self" consciousness, meaning that you lose track of your personal self and fully inhabit the role and the given circumstances. These are moments for the actor when you are "in the zone." They usually end with the actor saying, "What just happened? I know it was good, but what happened?" For actors, these moments are addictive. They are also elusive and the flow of such can be sometimes shut off by external factors—like the bored audience or the misplaced prop. Other times, these moments of connection can be shut off internally, and therein lies the roadblock.

Much has been written about neuroscience and its connection to peak performance, including using the nervous system to retrain the brain to allow easier access to peak performance levels. This work is fascinating and highly valued; however, this book examines the yet unidentified internal stratagems that create the roadblock for the individual. It is a system of identification and eradication of the roadblock in order to achieve the peak performance that actors seek. For more information on neuroscience and the ways it may relate to acting, look at Rhonda Blair's excellent book *The Actor, Image, and Action: Acting and Cognitive Neuroscience* and the writings and TED Talks of Dr. Sophie Scott, including her experiment with actress Fiona Shaw, examining what parts of the brain an actor uses when acting.

Dr. Moser, who works in the neuroscience research field, writes, "Neuroscience has lots of implications for what you focused on in this book, as it provides a window into the machinery that might be involved in the limitations we talked about. In general, neuroscience research on social anxiety and emotion regulation supports a lot of the interventions offered in this book." So, while this book does not explicitly examine the linkages between neuroscience and roadblocks, there are connections implicit in the strategies mentioned throughout the book. For deeper reading on social anxiety disorder (SAD) and emotional regulation, you may wish to examine the work of Dr. James Gross and Dr. Philippe Goldin.

The complex inner workings of the brain for most actors are most intimately connected to their inner monologue (or self-talk). This cognitive inner monologue (later transformed into that of character) offers us the closest most actors come to neuroscientific understanding of how your brain works. Use your inner monologue/self-talk skills to contemplate the exercises within this book. In this upcoming exercise, take the time to imagine the kind of actor you want to be. Examine the kind of work you want to do. List goals in your head. Write adjectives about your imagined work. Ruminate on the kind of actor you hope to become.

## Exercise 2.3   Define the kind of actor you want to be

### What Are the Patterns in Your Work?

The undertaking of active reflection in your work is the foundation for identifying any possible roadblocks in your craft. In order to provide you with a personal ownership of your craft and help yourself address roadblocks in your work, you must ultimately diminish your reliance on the validation or criticism of others. For now though, the ways in which others perceive your work are an important element in this initial investigative process.

In looking for patterns in your work, first try to identify through-lines or repeated issues from notes you have received from directors or in class. This moment of deep reflection, like the others earlier, is a chance for an evaluative and realistic overview of your craft. Again, your perception may be that you and a specific director had a bad working relationship or that your teacher gives positive comments regardless of your performance. This examination is just as much about negative notes as it is about praise. In terms of your acting, where do you consistently receive affirmation? Think also about the feedback you have received from peers, either in class, rehearsal, or at a post-rehearsal gathering. Start thinking and writing about notes that you recall from others. Include personal, seminal moments when you, as an actor, understood a concept, revealed a lapse in technique, or felt elated or humiliated based on the critique from others. If you are having trouble remembering the notes you receive from directors or teachers, begin to keep a record of all notes you collect, and spend some time reviewing them every few months in order to see what new patterns in your work are revealed. Start looking holistically at all of this collected information.

In putting together this collection of notes you may begin to see patterns emerge. As an example:

In voice class, I am always critiqued for speeding through my work.
In movement class, I am constantly being told to explore a concept with more patience and care.
My acting teacher is always telling me to breathe and let the moments land.
I am constantly being reminded to find my light and plant myself in the show I am currently rehearsing.
In other shows, I was told to stop clinging to the furniture and take my position down center.

I often receive praise for how great I am as an ensemble member and how thoughtful I am as a scene partner.

My fellow actors always mention how they love being around me in class because I have such a positive attitude.

In this scenario, you can start to see a pattern of an actor who lacks the confidence to command the attention he may richly deserve. His lack of confidence could have many origins: physical insecurities, comparing himself to peers, worrying about taking the time away from others, missing analysis of his work, feeling embarrassment about the high emotions in the role, understanding culturally that being "center stage" is selfish, or a host of other possibilities. Your current goal is not to diagnose the cause, but rather to begin to see patterns in your work.

## Exercise 2.4   Identify patterns in your work

Next, look at the type of roles that you have played in class, on stage, or on camera. Your casting in various roles can reveal a more complete critique of the way others perceive your professional self. Start to piece together the possible reasons behind this casting or the scene work you have done. Were you cast because of your look? Was this scene assigned in order to challenge you? Examine the material through the lens of the director who cast you or the teacher who assigned the work. If it is work you have chosen yourself, this can also be revealing.

You may find that you excel in a certain style or genre of performance. You may also find that you are more comfortable on screen than on stage. These personal comfort zones can also offer a jumping-off point for deeper examination. Why do these approaches to performing come more easily to you? An actor may want to be able to approach a Noël Coward comedy, a Sophocles tragedy, a commercial for toothpaste, an intimate film scene, or an experimental production with equal alacrity. And while such versatility is to be prized, for many actors a consistent roadblock may be viewed across various platforms. Examine your work related to style and variety.

Go back and scour published reviews of your acting or written assessments of past performance work. This can include anything from reviews published online, Facebook posts in which your performance may have been tagged, or an old critique from a competition in high school. These written reviews can remind you of things you may have forgotten. Even if you disagree with a review, this is a way to ascertain another's relatively detached opinion.

## Exercise 2.5    Examine the type of work you do

Take a good look at your résumé. First, look over the general quality and lay-out. What does it say about you as an actor? Is it sleek and organized or overly packed with loads of information? How are you marketing yourself? Does it look professional? Have you not found the time to do the revision you know you need? Then look at the roles you have performed and identify whether you think they were a success or a struggle. Why did you succeed in this role and not that one? What might this reveal about you? Deep reflection about the terms "successful" and "struggle" is required. Do a great review and an au-dience's laughter qualify success, even if you felt the performance lacked hon-esty? If you were experimenting in your craft and making bold new choices that the audience felt did not quite work, is that role considered a struggle?

## Exercise 2.6    Identify the successes and struggles on your résumé

Finally, think about your reputation as an actor. What do you think people say about you in casting sessions, post-rehearsal, or outside of class? Con-sider the positives and negatives. What would someone say about you if it came down to casting you or another actor in a role? What is your contri-bution to that reputation? Are you funny in rehearsal but lacking in disci-pline? Are you so focused on the work that you forget to enjoy the process? Examine this idea of reputation in detail.

## Exercise 2.7    Examine your reputation

It must be reiterated that, throughout this chapter, all of the exercises are aimed at examining your reason for acting and your relationship to the craft. They force deeper reflection than most actors tend to regularly give their work. The goal of these investigations may reveal alignments and revelations related to the actor you were, the actor you are, and the actor you want to become.

In this next exercise, seek out the opinion of others in person. Ask your peers, educators, or directors what they think of your work. Begin to keep a record of how others honestly assess your work—the pros and the cons. Try to remove any defense when gathering the information, but rather look at the feedback as a chance to immediately examine how others perceive what you are do-ing. This exercise might sting to hear or read immediate holistic critique, but in the spirit of gathering all of the necessary data, you must try to directly examine how others perceive your work with a dispassionate removal of ego.

## Exercise 2.8    Have others share opinions of your work

All of the data you have collected can inform this next exercise in which you will write a short biography of yourself. The bio offers a chance to put together all of the elements of this chapter. Why did you start to act? What type of actor are you? What are some of your struggles and successes in certain roles? This bio should be written in the third person because this idea of distancing yourself from your work (covered later in this chapter) offers proven benefits. Below are three examples from a few actors (their names have been removed and replaced with "—"). Think of it as your bio for a playbill, an award, or your Wikipedia page.

## Exercise 2.9    Write a bio

Here is a bio from a student freshly exploring the concept of roadblocks:

*Audiences are captivated by the energy that — presents on stage. A native of Metro-Detroit, — made her first claim to fame in various local church plays, lighting up newspapers with her smile each year. She later discovered her love for performing during her time in high school musicals where she performed in ensembles for shows like* Oklahoma! *and* Jekyll & Hyde. *The dark side of a show such as* Jekyll *allowed — to act freely and develop a character in the ensemble, which she thinks helped her to later land the role of Hope Harcourt in* Anything Goes. *This role solidified her adoration for musical theater. A memorable moment in her career was her first rehearsal for* Anything Goes *where her director stopped her before she even spoke, expressing that he did not want to see her typical ingénue style, stripping — of her type. The challenges in her development of this role were eased with acceptance from her peers and audiences. While attending college, — took a break from musical theater to pursue other roles including Julie in Neil Simon's,* Jake's Women, *where she played the antagonizing ghost of Jake's late wife. In this role, — struggled with the vulnerability and emotion related to her need for attention and acceptance. Her latest roles include Constance in* Station to Station, *a one-act presented in the Student Playwright Series. This particular role, as the flighty, unpredictable Constance, challenged — to physically explore the imaginary worlds illustrated in the script and challenged her as she had to develop an imaginary relationship with her conservative husband. She is currently focused on doing more authentic work, keeping it separate from her messy personal life, and shedding habits of indicating and overperforming. — hopes that this effort will help her to discover more about herself as an actor and an individual.*

Here is a bio from an actor who classifies himself as a character actor:

*— (b. December 19, 1994) is a young American actor. He was born in Saginaw, Michigan, and started his acting career performing in various productions at Heritage High School. As an actor — has found himself succeeding in roles that called him to dive deep into the characterization process, gaining him much acclaim as a character actor. In the past, he has played various roles such as The White Rabbit in* Alice's Adventures in Wonderland, *Blackbeard the Pirate in* A Night at the Wax Museum, *Feargal in* Back to the 80s, *Mr. Collins in* Pride and Prejudice, *and Cinderella's Prince/The Wolf in Sondheim's* Into the Woods. *Being a more transformative actor — found difficulty in his early years adapting to roles that did not require serious alterations to his own character. His performance as Hugo Peabody in the musical* Bye, Bye Birdie *lacked connection and tends to get overshadowed by his more successful character work. While this role was one of his more forgettable, it did give him the confidence and experience he needed to move on to his more memorable roles: Feargal, Mr. Collins, Blackbeard, etc.*

And one final bio that uses a highly analytic approach:

*— is an actor who has made her career successfully portraying characters who exhibit a narrow range of appropriate emotional responses. In his book* Teaching with Poverty in Mind, *Eric Jensen describes the emotional and social deficits of children raised in poverty. Borrowing from Ekman, he points out that the brains of infants are hardwired for only six emotions: joy, anger, surprise, disgust, sadness, and fear (Ekman, 2003). As an actor, — has been able to master expressing these basic emotions. She struggles, however, to portray characters who exhibit many of the emotional responses that must be explicitly taught to children and are often missing in the training of children raised in poverty. Some of these emotions can be found on the "emotional keyboard" and they include humility, forgiveness, empathy, optimism, compassion, sympathy, patience, shame, cooperation, and gratitude (Jensen, 2009). Though — was raised in a middle-class home, her parents were influenced by generational poverty and did not do much training regarding emotional responses. As a result, — has not felt comfortable playing roles where her character is loving or in love because in*

*the playing of those types of roles, those "taught" emotions would have to be tapped. She has had success in roles where her character was funny, or again, expressing those basic emotions. These struggles were evident in her recent portrayal of Laurinda in the play,* The Summer Circle. *In this role, — played a child who was bossy, but not mean, and self-absorbed, yet friendly. — struggled to embody the nuances of this character, finding it easier to make her unlikeable rather than adorable. In the scenes of the play where —'s character was comedic, she was more comfortable and felt more successful with these moments. Similarly, in the play* 100 Saints You Should Know *by Kate Fodor, — struggled to convey the complexity of a mother who finds herself coping with the choices her adult son has made and the consequences of those choices. — was challenged to portray the layers of compassion, shame, empathy, forgiveness, and ultimately, gratitude that her character experienced. Ultimately, as an actor, — is capable of achieving notes but challenged with striking chords.*

While the first two bios have a sense of humor to them, they also reveal an understanding of where these actors are in this investigative process and begin to hint at possible roadblocks. The third goes deeper and more obviously connects to an ingrained roadblock. Perhaps the first actor's struggle with vulnerability is connected to her need for acceptance. Perhaps the second actor's love of transformative acting and struggles with personal acting on stage hints that he is lacking truth in his work. Perhaps the third actor's lack of emotional range is related to fear. These roadblocks are implied in the ways in which the three actors share the information about themselves. Review your bio for clues about what you choose to share and what you choose to avoid.

The importance of writing in the third person is something that all consultants offered as a compelling way to keep actors safe in either preparing for or reflecting on a performance. The research of Ozlem Ayduk and Ethan Kross (2015) has found great benefits for self-talk in the third person. They write, "Our findings are just a small part of a much larger, ongoing stream of research on self-talk, which is proving to have far-reaching implications for altering the way people think, feel, and behave. Not only does non-first-person self-talk help people perform better under stress and help them get control of their emotions, it also helps them reason more wisely."

From Figure 2.1, you can see the proven benefits of such a strategy. Expanding this idea for an actor whose entire career depends on self-talk (at rehearsal, auditions, or performance) may reduce anxiety at these already stressful situations. Third-person writing and self-talk are imperative for the actor.

Kross and Ayduk's fascinating work (see, for example, Kross and Ayduk, 2011; Kross et al., 2014; Ayduk and Kross, 2015) has deeply affected how I set goals in rehearsal and in the studio. I ask actors to speak about prepara-

**PRONOUNS MATTER WHEN PSYCHING YOURSELF UP**
People who thought about themselves in the second or third  person before giving a speech turned in better performance and ruminated less afterward than those who thought in the first person.

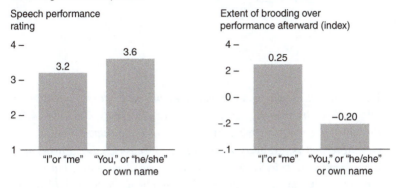

**Figure 2.1   Self-talk graph (from Ayduk and Kross, 2015)**

Source: Ethan Kross, Ozlem Ayduk, and the Journal of Personality and Social Psychology in the *Harvard Business Review*

tion by speaking in the third person. For example, based on the bio of the first actor, their goal in the run of the play tonight will be "For — to access her vulnerability by concentrating on her scene partner and not the audience's reaction like she normally does." Or the second actor might say, "— is going to avoid using his usual tricks when approaching this scene in order to find the honesty." Or the final actor might state, "— is going to seek out other notes available on her emotional keyboard." This one little augmentation to the preparation and reflection process has reduced stress before and after presentations and performances.

You may note that the entire chapter has strongly avoided any examination of your personal self and was only an examination of yourself as actor. As you begin to gather this information, you may be alarmed to note that the patterns, types, struggles, successes, and feedback may have resonance in your personal life. An ability to maintain a separation between these crossovers is covered in Chapter 3.

By deeply reflecting on your work, approach, process, successes, struggles, and reputation, you should have a clear idea of who you are as an actor. While you may begin to see patterns that hint at possible roadblocks, the goal of this chapter was to explore your professional self in relation to your craft. And although you may have already started to process some of the information, your work has just begun.

# 3     Understanding Your Other Selves

*We started with taking notes on ourselves, our personal self, professional self, motivations, interests, strengths, weaknesses, habits, and so on. After this free-form self-assessment, we moved on to calculated assessments on introversion vs. extroversion and the Big Five personality traits. These assessments only reflected what I already knew about myself but maybe not to the same degree. I discovered that I am highly introverted both personally and professionally, I am only moderately open to new experiences, and I am alarmingly neurotic. All of these traits directly relate to my roadblock, which has negatively affected my work for far too long. My constant need to perfectly replicate each moment in a performance from the night before dulls my choices and creates a shallow product. I could never "live in the moment" or "dirty my work" because my mind could not let me relax or find new moments for fear of seeming unprofessional. This whole process has felt somewhat like rehab and the roadblock is like an addiction.*

In Chapter 2 you examined your professional self. In this chapter, the investigation will expand to other areas. You will first explore the linkage between your personal self and your professional self. The examination will then expand to those selves in relation to the characters you create. Through the use of standardized assessments, you may begin to examine the intersection of these three areas.

There is you as an actor and there is you as a person. One is your job and one is who you are away from your job. It may appear easy to understand the delineation between your occupation and your personal life. You are not your job. And it is simple to imagine that your personal life may have a more relaxed quality than your ambitious professional life or similar distinctions. But as Dr. Jason Moser explains, there are more crossovers than you might think: "There is professional self and personal self. Do those values always correlate? Should they? People who succeed in business usually have an organized quality and actors have that crossover too. Generally, actors are highly emotional and highly anxious people." These qualities are both demanded by and resultant from the profession. Dr. Moser explains, "Their internal focus causes anxiety, and similarly, they can be highly critical of self and others because of constant self-examination. In most cases, actors are highly matched in personal and professional self. Actors are obvious, transparent personalities spending their time exploring emotion."

As an actor, you may also use your personal life in order to inform your professional life. In many approaches to acting, you begin your work with the usual question of, "What if I (personally) was in this character's situation?" From the first moments of plying your trade, you have blended your personal and professional selves. The commingling of selves can be confusing, dangerous, or rewarding. But careful attention and a clear understanding of which self is being employed are necessary for an actor's wellbeing.

## Who Are You? (Self)

The ancient Greek dictum "Know Thyself" is an imperative for all but is especially true for actors. As an actor you must understand who you are as an individual before you can begin to examine and inhabit the role of another. While you may pretend to understand yourself, most actors rarely take the necessary time to examine their personal self and how it affects their professional work, and, by extension, how their personal self seeps (despite your best efforts) into the characters they portray. Even if your approach to acting limits your personal connection to the character, you may begin to see patterns emerge related to the outcome of your final performances.

Going back to your basis for acting, you may see a connection between personal and professional self, either through seeking attention or finding an escape. The two types of actors identified in the previous chapter also have a blending of selves. Personality actors fully use their personal selves in relation to the professional selves' analysis of given circumstances. Character actors transform their professional selves, although you also see the basic humanity of their personal selves peek through. While the personal and professional are inextricably linked, they are also distinctive.

An interesting exchange occurred when Dr. Moser visited the class related to the interconnectedness of professional and personal self.

I included the entire transcript since I think it also has valuable information related to creating boundaries, goals, and definitions:

**Student:** I have a really hard time working with people professionally if I don't have a personal connection with them. If I don't feel that they like me or if I feel that I don't like them, I get really stressed out about it and can't do what I need to do.

**Moser:** I would like to ask the question, "Why?" I think trying to understand why that might be the case would be a really useful place to start. Just in terms of trying to understand what professionalism means to you. What does professional versus personal mean to you as a concept? Maybe you don't have a sense of those things being different. Maybe personal or professional will never be different for you. In order for you to be successful, this is what you're going to need. That's just your comfort zone; that's your cognitive set point. We all have varying set points of where we like to hover around in terms of our experience. Maybe you value personal connection above all else. If that's such a core value for you, and you put that at the top, above all else, then that is a precondition for everything else that is going to follow. But what if you didn't have this personal relationship, and you just keep that professional? How might that look? Would that be OK? How would you feel? What if you never really knew how they felt about you as a person? Could you accept that? And if you can, then you can separate professional and personal relationships. You may continue to say, "My professional self will always be more vulnerable than my personal self. I don't value vulnerability personally as much as I value some other things." Then that's fine. You have defined those areas and your needs.

To help keep a clearer delineation of professional and personal self, you can use assessments. The upcoming test is your first foray into standardized and readily available testing. While you may think that this is nothing more than a Facebook poll on someone's newsfeed, I was directed to these specific diagnostic tests by the consultants in this book. They praised the immediacy of the results and noted that these are some of the same questionnaires that their patients are asked to fill out. Another added benefit is that you can gain concrete evidence related to your approach to acting.

Using accepted and standardized tests to explore the various versions of self is something Dr. Chris Hopwood championed in order to examine the various selves of the actor. Like his work in psychology, the assessments are a way to quickly begin the conversation about personal core issues or, in our case, roadblocks in our professional work. He suggests, "We use the data from the assessments and organize it around a principal question so that we can easily focus on a core issue. It's a kind of a collaborative thing where you try not to be the expert but we let the patient be the expert, kind of the driver, so they can become curious about the question." In your case, the question you seek the answer to is, "What is my roadblock in acting?" Or, "Do I even have a roadblock?" The upcoming tests are a chance for you to become more intimately aware of your personal contribution to the work you perform in your professional life.

As with all self-reporting, there are wild variables, including your inference of the wording of the question, your mood that day, your commitment to the process, the lack of clarification in the questions, and the absence of nuanced response. All of these, and any other issues, are valid. In his eloquent article, "A Process Dissociation Approach to Objective-Projective Test Score Interrelationships," Dr. Robert Bornstein examines the flaws and variables in such testing. Despite these variables, the ubiquitous nature of the tests and their immediate calculations make this an easy starting place for personal examination. Dr. Chris Hopwood also cautions that, "Clinically, one trick we use when looking at scales on tests—like the ones you are using—is how defensive the person is. How much does the person exaggerate? And that's why we have those scales to say, 'Well we know what the person's clinical profile looks like. How much do we think that's true?'" Your work will be shared with no one other than yourself, so aim for complete honesty in your responses.

You will be using the Big Five/Five Factor Model (FFM) Personality Test as the basis for most of your exploration. This assessment is a series of questions related to five broad areas or traits including extroversion, agreeableness, conscientiousness, neuroticism, and openness to experience. The questions contained within each section were created to explore the wide variability within personality types. This commonly used test will offer you a clear way in which to analyze your work.

You will take this test several times. The first assessment is solely related to your personal self. Who are you at home? With friends? With a lover? Alone? Who are you when stripped of your professional worries?

## Exercise 3.1    Big Five FFM as personal self

The test in Exercise 3.1 is easily found in several places online but is most easily available at the following site: www.outofservice.com/bigfive/

This site offers immediate results that may or may not surprise you. The goal here is to get a sense of self that is easily understandable and categorized. The completed version of these tests need not be shared with anyone, as this is work that will allow you to discover more about your individual process. Examine the results for any discrepancies related to your expectations. Dr. Chris Hopwood spoke about the process of reading this data: "I see it as an evolving process where you are going to test these results out about yourself in some situations to see whether your reading of your data—or even if the data itself—is relevant in cross situations or not. I'd be curious how you evolve in your self concept." This concept of evolution related to the information you receive is quite important. As you take the test through various lenses, the data will become multidimensional, offering a more complex examination of your work. Please note that I have opted not to use information that students self-reported on these assessments, as the process is highly personal. I will, however, share what the majority of actors discovered, as well as possible reasons for results that landed in the minority.

For myself, I was surprised that when I took the test my conscientiousness score was unexpectedly low. Upon further reflection, I realized that my lack of patience (something I don't necessarily like about myself) was the root of that score. I had to come to terms with the fact that, although I do not enjoy that aspect within me, it is a powerful part of my personal self. When you look over the results try to remain objective and open.

## Who Are You? (Actor)

As an actor, you are a unique breed who spends your time doing things most others try to avoid. Who in their right mind would want to be on display in front of an audience facing judgment? Who wants to spend time examining deeply complex emotional material in order to "bring it to life"? Who wants to play another character when they have enough trouble figuring out themselves? Dr. Moser understands this unique aspect and thinks it is important to get:

> a grounded sense of yourself and a strong perspective about what you are going to take on in your job. What is different from the work that I do is that I'm dealing with people who are having these things happen

to them, and they don't want them. But you [as actors] are inviting them. You are inviting these emotions. You are saying, "I want to have these things that may feel really bad. Because I need to do it to access this role." So you are inviting these things on purpose, lots of the people that I work with don't want anything to do with those feelings.

What becomes obvious is that every actor's unique slant on life requires a unique way to examine that life. Any approach to acting still demands an understanding of what makes a character "tick" and these tests can showcase if you are creating similar internal mechanisms for varied characters.

Understanding who you are as an individual is key to being a good actor (or educator). How can you play someone else if you do not know who you are? You are an individual with three separate and distinct selves (self, actor, and character). Dr. Hopwood understands the need for self-actualization as actor noting, "As an actor, I feel it is extremely important to know yourself and recognize patterns in your work—meaning if I do not really know my own self reasonably well, I'm going to be a part of the pattern, and I'm not going to be able to figure out the difference between the pattern and me." One way to achieve an intimate knowledge of all three selves is through the systematic approach to roadblocks.

To that end, in this upcoming assessment, you will investigate your professional and not your personal self. You will answer the questions only from your career perspective. The professional self for the actor means the public face that you present at networking events, auditions, in the rehearsal studio, and on the film set. It is also related to your work ethic in regard to preparation for auditions, script analysis for rehearsal, and the ways in which you manage your career. You may call yourself a "lazy" person but may still be highly motivated related to your profession.

### Exercise 3.2   Big Five FFM as professional self

Look first at the results of this test (Exercise 3.2) and for any anomalies between your expectations and your results related to your professional self. If possible, identify why that occurred. Then compare the results of the two versions of the assessments (personal and professional) side by side. What are the similarities and what are the differences?

You may find that there are distinct areas of difference, but most likely, you will see a major connection between personal and professional self. As explained earlier in relation to the general disposition of actors as well as the use of self in professional work, similarly corresponding scores across the testing are usually the case. In most categories, a majority of actors found that, although some minor discrepancies occurred, their personal and professional selves aligned within 15 points difference in their percentiles. Those who found larger differences identified a stronger understanding and sense of separation between personal and professional self.

For myself I found my major differences were the introversion/extroversion percentiles (with a difference of over 50 points) and my conscientiousness percentiles (nearly a 40-point difference). In my analysis of the data, that makes perfect sense to me. I have cultivated a more extroverted and organized demeanor in my professional life than I possess in my personal life. And while my introversion and my lack of patience are parts of my everyday life, my professional life has been crafted to amplify those particular qualities I see necessary for success. You too can begin to adapt or augment the personal elements that may impede your professional self. Should your scores, like mine, vary widely in any of the categories, spend time examining that discrepancy and find its root.

## Are You an Extroverted or Introverted Actor?

In Susan Cain's bestseller *Quiet: The Power of Introverts in a World That Can't Stop Talking,* and in her TED Talks, she describes the stigma that comes with the word "introvert." Introverts have been described as shy, reserved, or slower rather than that which they truly are—private, introspective, and thoughtful. She calls for a restructuring of business and educational practices where the loudest or first voice to answer usually wins. A similar reformation of theatrical practices might also be in order. As an introvert myself, I know the panic that ensues when anyone mentions improvisation or the dread I feel when heading to a networking event. I also envy the extroverts who thrive in improvisational play or see networking as a chance to meet like-minded professionals. In many sections of this book you can examine the impact of current theatrical training on introverted actors, but for now, let's accept these general classifications and examine how they can align with some of the exercises in Chapter 2. In a tidy world, the actor who went into acting to gain attention would be a personality actor who is an extrovert. Likewise, in a tidy world, an actor who went into acting to lose herself would be a character actor who is introverted. But while these answers usually do fall along these lines, the world is not always tidy.

You can be a dependable and extroverted actor professionally and an introverted individual personally. As mentioned, my work as director and educator has created a professional self of extroversion in production or class, while my personal life is that of introversion. More commonly, though, actors are either introverted or extroverted human beings and can be similarly categorized related to their professional selves. As all of us have both qualities within us (ambiverts), you must define the majority of your work as actor in one category—introvert or extrovert. While you may balk at this simple categorization, it is another chance to examine the process. You may also feel that these personal tests have little to do with how you approach acting, but, remember, external outputs such as work ethic, commitment, and physicality are all implicit within the test's findings.

Take the assessment below twice; first as self and then as actor. There are many introvert/extrovert assessments online, but this one was recommended by the consultants and can be found here: http://psychologytoday.tests.psychtests.com/take_test.php?idRegTest= 1311

## Exercise 3.3    Are you introvert or extrovert? (Personal self)

## Exercise 3.4    Are you introvert or extrovert? (Professional self)

When taking the test as your personal self, you may find that some questions specifically ask you about your professional self or how others perceive you at work. Use you best judgment in answering these questions. When taking this assessment, you are forced to begin to create clearer delineations related to the two selves. Again, the majority of students found similarities between both scores with variances between 10 and 20 points. My scores were separated between the two versions of the tests by over 50 points. Given my cultivation of distinct personal and professional selves, the variance makes perfect sense.

At this point, you may be feeling overwhelmed and overanalytical with all of the testing or you may be energized by the information you are receiving. Whatever the case, you must remember that you are seeking clarification for where your work may be hindered by a roadblock. The information you are gathering may be causing stress or may seem too interesting not to tell others. You may share some of the confusion or discoveries with your peers or teacher if you think it will help.

Should the actor wish to share information with them, Marika Reisberg has some guidance for educators: "You follow the student's lead in this. There are ways to invite the conversations should you see the need. Students are juggling lots of information. And depending on your knowledge of their work, and the fact that you do know them so well, it can create a sense of cohesion to the investigative process."

## Who Are You? (Character)

The unique life of an actor requires an integral task of compartmentalizing. You have explored the undeniable relationship between your personal and professional selves, but what makes an actor inimitable is the third self—that of character. Only an actor creates and lives in the skin of this third self. Even if that skin is layered on externally in your approach to acting, looking at the physical and external similarities can offer clues or reveal limitations across the range of characters you portray. In this section, you will examine the correlation between all three selves. The nexus of these three areas is where an actor must spend time examining the wanted or unwanted crossover that may most perceptibly impede your craft. Dr. Moser notes, "The issue becomes the introduction of character to the mix. They must have the tools to distinguish between selves and character." It is in this interface of the three areas where acting lies. The goal is to become a consummate professional and to understand how all three selves intersect. This will allow you to become a more adept actor and explore work that is currently impeded by personal barriers.

How you view the intersection of selves between actor, professional, and character can be as varied as the perceived difference between personality and character acting. When looking at a role, you might begin with the personal self, perhaps having a visceral, individual reaction to the script. Then, the professional self enters and interacts with the personal as you begin to employ investigative techniques—"Under what circumstances could I be in the position?"; "How would I react in this situation?"; "What would make me have a similar response?" The blending of these two selves—the emotional personal reaction to the role and the analytical professional self—can be blurry as the emotional storehouse is most logically within the personal self. How, then, can you access those emotions while remaining personally healthy? This is where the character enters the intricate world. You will use the core of your personal self for each role, in combination with your professional skills. Based on your understanding of the script, you will then choose what aspects of your personal self to enhance to create the third self, the character who "lives" in the world of the play or film. The character will be feeling the giddy highs of new love and the darkest despair of a bitter divorce—not you. The character has to have access to all of the emotions that the screenwriter and playwright demand. The character will be the one in dangerous, deeply emotional, high-stakes, dramatic situations that create the best entertainment. You may keep your "selves" better compartmentalized and more emotionally healthy if you can create a clearly defined approach to your way of acting across the three categories.

That compartmentalization requires an individual understanding of the human mind. Acting and psychology expert Dr. Thalia R. Goldstein recognizes the uniquely personal relationship the actor has to psychology when creating a character: "Actors are unique to study because their job *is* psychology, made flesh. Their job is to understand why people have the beliefs, desires, emotions, behaviors that they do, and then turn that understanding into an embodiment that is easily read by an audience." She avows a deeper understanding of others is necessary in order to act in relation to an audience's acceptance of believable emotional response. Dr. Goldstein continues, "So it's even more than simple understanding because they have to translate it for themselves *and* translate it for their audience. Their knowledge of psychology is personal in a way that a psychologist's knowledge isn't. And they do it over and over for different characters." In this last quote, creating a personal approach to embodying unique characters with unique motivations seems key. It is crucial to make sure that you understand yourself while, at the same time, you should recognize that each person, and therefore each character, is individual. Even if you don't subscribe to Dr. Goldstein's (and this book's) assumption that acting and psychology are linked, you may recognize that an actor's personal, individual psychology does influence their commitment to non-psychologically based acting.

We read about and lionize actors who "stay in character" for the entire shoot—those actors who must "live the role" in order to achieve it. In this equation, the blending of character self and actor self seems more important than the personal self. Some actors don't have the time or inclination for such an approach. Conversely, some actors shrug off any pretense of character and offer their approach as, "I was just being me." The character self is removed from this equation in favor of professional and personal. Between these two extremes lives your approach to acting. Finding the distribution of personal, professional, and characters selves is an individual formula. You can define your approach to acting by the percentages and protocols in which you use the three selves.

Finding clarity and moving between these three selves is imperative for an actor. Think about a rehearsal and the juggling of your many selves. You are rehearsing a scene (character), stopping for adjustments from the director (professional), moving back into the scene (character), and then the stage manager announces a break and you phone your friend (personal). Dr. Moser suggests practicing this exchanging of selves to acquire more alacrity, thereby gaining a deeper understanding of them. He advises that you may become better at compartmentalizing through this repetition. Dr. Moser notes, "I think you have to work out these muscles, and you have to do the best you can in identifying your comfort zone and a range of your comfort zone from the easiest thing for you to do. 'I'm in and out of this character with no problem, this character is sort of like myself, no big deal. I can play that and still know who I am personally.'"

Not much is known about the relationship of the actor and three selves because as Dr. Moser notes, "We do some of this research in the lab and unfortunately, for [actors], the state of the research has so much focus on decreasing negative emotions. So much of the research says, 'Let's bring it down' where [actors] are trying to bring it up and explore it across various means." So it again hands the approach to the individual actor to refine and distill your process.

In Chapter 2, you were asked to examine the work on your résumé and past scene work to identify struggles and successes related to your acting. You should approach the next exercise armed with that recent examination. Now you must reenter the mindset of two characters that you have felt the most and least successful with in class or in rehearsal. Of course, it would help if these were recent incarnations. In taking these two versions of the test, don't answer externally how the audience or your analysis perceived the role, but rather, how the character perceives herself. So while Malvolio in *Twelfth Night* may appear to be tense, cold, and aloof to the audience and to the other characters in the play, this is not what he thinks of himself. Using the characters' core values, beliefs, and emotional complexities, answer the assessment first as a character you felt was a success and then, aligning your thoughts with that of the character you felt was a struggle, take the test again.

## Exercise 3.5   Big Five FFM as character you felt successful in portraying

## Exercise 3.6   Big Five FFM as character you felt you struggled in portraying

Compare the first two Big Five Assessments—personal self (Exercise 3.1) and professional self (Exercise 3.2)—with the iterations of Exercises 3.5 and 3.6 and look for similarities and divergence. You may find that the role that you struggled with most sharply contrasts with your personal self. It is most likely that you find yourself more comfortable and more successful in work that tests similarly to you. In our tidy world, you might see that your extroverted, highly open to new experiences self aligns with your personality acting and you felt most successful playing a heightened version of your real self. Or that your introverted, highly neurotic and conscientious self aligns with your character acting and that you struggled most with a role that was too similar to you personally. But alas, the world is not tidy. And that is where the roadblock may lie.

In my reading of the data from my four versions of the Big Five/FFM tests, two interesting patterns revealed themselves. My results in the "calm/relaxed" versus "nervous/high-strung" were consistent through three versions of the test (self, professional, and character I felt I portrayed successfully. My scores were quite high in the "nervous/high strung" area, with slight differences in the percentile. The character I struggled with was at the other end of the spectrum by a wide margin, landing firmly in the "calm/relaxed area." There was a difference of nearly 80 points. My reading of that information revealed that perhaps I rely on speed or high-strung characters similar to my own tempo. This is a very common problem.

In tandem with the information collected in the introvert/extrovert assessment, another issue I noted was my firm delineations of introvert in personal life and extrovert in professional life; my characters had similar disparities. The character I succeeded with was defined as a very strong ex-

**Table 3.1    Results from the standardized tests**

|  | Open to Experiences | Conscientiousness | Extroversion | Agreeableness | Neuroticism |
|---|---|---|---|---|---|
| Self | 85 | 40 | 25 | 85 | 92 |
| Professional | 93 | 89 | 78 | 79 | 85 |
| Character Success | 7 | 74 | 87 | 63 | 87 |
| Character Struggle | 20 | 89 | 16 | 57 | 10 |

trovert, while the character I struggled with was defined as an introvert. Looking back over my résumé, I can see that pattern repeated. What is my relationship to creating extroverted or introverted characters? Do I avoid introspection on stage but value it in real life? Armed with this information, I can continue on with more focused areas of attention.

Your reading of your results can reveal similar information. You may even wish to create a table like that of Table 3.1 to assist you in processing all of the information gathered in these assessments in order to see it more clearly. Simply place your percentile scores from each version and look for clues. You can expand your table with other characters that you have played in performance or class or even characters you dream of playing. Try to examine all of the data gathered in a way that is most helpful for you.

In looking at the information presented in Table 3.1, you may more readily see the discrepancies I mentioned related to neuroticism and extroversion. Some areas to also examine could be that, despite my openness to new experiences in life, people may think I succeed in roles that have a more traditional view of the world related to the scores in the "Open to Experiences" column. In looking over my résumé, I can see that this is just something these two characters have in common and most likely is not a through-line in my work. Another area to examine may be the agreeableness scores that are consistent across all four versions. Do I only play characters that are likable? This very natural tendency may be somewhat true in looking at other work I have done, but it is not a major influence in my choices. This may be something to examine in concert with my reliance on high-strung characters and my inability for true introspection on stage.

Your reading of your information may be similarly editorial. You may see some information as an anomaly related to the character. You may find some interesting patterns that aren't relevant to your work. Most important for our purposes, you may also find patterns that are entirely relevant to what currently affects your acting.

Examine the roles or types of roles you are most desperate to play (Exercise 3.7). Examine them first as archetype—are they a stock character or do any characteristic patterns emerge? Do you always want to play the outsider with a dangerous gleam in his eye? Next, examine them related to the data. Are those roles in direct opposition or are they completely congruous to the work you normally do? Do you want to play the outsider because it aligns with information from your table? Or do you want to play the mysterious outsider because it is something far removed from your usual roles where you only play the nice guy?

## Exercise 3.7  What are your dream roles?

At this point, the reasons for these assessments should be clear to you, as your gathering of data can begin to reveal patterns related to your acting. You also may find the tests too time-consuming or unrelatable in their focus. You may wish to choose a shorter one to speed up the process or act as a shorthand for experimentation, such as the "Acceptance and Action Questionnaire" (Hayes et al., 2006) Or you may find you can more easily relate to the Myers–Briggs Type Indicator (MBTI). You could even create your own shorthand test to make sure that, when acting, you have not fallen into patterns by asking limited and targeted questions. Regardless of which test you take, the data for reflection is what matters most.

As you have skillfully examined your process and past work, you have begun to take responsibility for your craft. You should have a clear idea of patterns in both the struggles and the success in your work. You also have a clear assessment of your three selves—personal, professional, and character. You are now ready to begin to identify your roadblock in acting.

# 4    Identifying Roadblocks

*What I can say most about roadblocks is that they are fluid. They are constructed in the mind, even if they manifest as physical limitations with embodying a character, and the process of overcoming one is a process of undoing patterns of the self. With the personality tests we took during the beginning of the year, as actor and as person, it is true that we may have different behavior patterns when playing each role, but ultimately, the person behind the actor's role—the experiences they have had which inform their behavior (and shape their thought process), their personal creative fire, and the ways they have learned to respond under pressure—is where roadblocks begin.*

There are many self-help books that talk about the self-imposed barriers that athletes place on their performance, most notably W. Timothy Gallwey's original *The Inner Game of Tennis,* published in 1974. It was one of the first books to recognize that the mind can impede performance. Gallwey's notion that anxiety and self-doubt can affect the potential and talent of the athlete pioneered sports psychology and paved the way for a string of subsequent self-help books such as *The Inner Game of Skiing, The Inner Game of Golf,* and even *The Inner Game of Music.* Like any athlete, an actor is also playing an inner game within his mind that allows for distracted or negative thoughts of forgotten lines, missed cues, lost laughs, and physical insecurities, when the focus should remain on the outer game—the scene partner. This negatively tinged inner game is enmeshed with roadblocks, and it is up to you to identify and extinguish them. Your goal is for an inner game that allows positive thought.

## What Is a Roadblock?

A roadblock is an issue or issues that prevent(s) an actors from doing their best work. It prevents you from being the agile and versatile vessel for human expression, on stage or on screen. It impedes your main job, which is to represent truthful human behavior. Or, if you are acting in a genre that does not value realism, it may impact your ability to commit fully to the style. A roadblock can be psychological or physical. A roadblock can be a lack of knowledge or a willful disregard of information. As mentioned earlier, for the purposes of this book, a roadblock is not a lack of skills; it is a psychologically based impediment to your best work. A roadblock is personal.

A roadblock in an actor's work is a common and ever-shifting concern that can be either resolved easily or camouflaged until you can more readily address the issue; it can remain ignored or lessened over time through strategy. These strategies include confronting the issue head on through aggressive and targeted exercises, taking smaller incremental steps to outsmart it, or simply acknowledging the roadblock. Your ultimate hope is that, over time, the roadblock may decrease and therefore lessen its power on your work. Roadblocks are deeply rooted in the personal psyche but manifest themselves in the actor and character selves. A roadblock is something that actors want to remove in order to unfetter their work.

Dr. Chris Hopwood explains the impact of an actor's roadblock on their work: "If you have to do a certain role, you have to somewhat feel what the character is feeling, and you have to access a version of that feeling in yourself. If there is a roadblock to that feeling, it seems like it would be extremely difficult to do." Hopwood draws parallels between an actor's roadblock and the barriers his students face in a clinic he supervises, as various patients need distinct qualities from the student therapists. Sometimes the psychology students, like the actor, are unable to produce the necessary emotional qualities and recognize their personal roadblocks.

The data provided in Chapter 3 reveal a roadblock of reliance on speed and high energy in order to avoid introspection. This is a very common issue for actors. You will read examples of many roadblock statements later in this chapter, but for now, look at three possibilities related to a single roadblock. For example, an actor is tired of playing only comedic roles, but when those dramatic roles are provided, they paralyze the actor in one of three ways; either:

(1) because he wants to perform this kind of work so badly.

OR

(2) because he keeps thinking of the scenes only as a comedy.

OR

    (3) because he is unable to tap into honest interaction and ends up pushing, like he does in a comedic role.

His roadblock may be:

    (1) he currently lacks the skills to perform drama.

OR

    (2) his safest place is understandably where he has found the most success.

OR

    (3) he has real trouble accessing honesty on stage.

Solutions to those roadblocks could include:

    (1) a repetition of a variety of dramatic scene work until he gains those skills.

OR

    (2) a reframing of his analytical skills to find the dramatic conflict.

OR

    (3) a focus on interior work to access vulnerability.

The actor must examine the self-identified issue "I'm tired of playing only comedic roles" from various vantage points. Jonathon Novello states, "A roadblock related to an actor can either be accepted ('I'm fine with comedy being my thing') or be a dissatisfaction ('I wish I could tackle more dramatic roles'). It is within this dissatisfaction that the actor must tackle the roadblock." If we look at the same issue from an "outside in" perspective, the question broadens to, "What barriers have I created to prevent me from finding more physical freedom?" If you seek to expand this or any portion of your acting work using this emotionally based approach, you must address your roadblock.

    It should be noted again that not all actors have a roadblock or wish to address one they consider to be benign. Some fear that the roadblock is what makes them unique. They fear its removal, like in Oliver Sacks' case study "Witty Ticcy Ray," a story about a gifted drummer with Tourette's syndrome who, when medicated, felt that his musical gifts had been taken away. Sometimes the roadblock is so ingrained that it has become part of our standard performance.

On a visit to an acting class, Dr. Moser responded to some questions from students exploring roadblocks in their work and spoke about how not all actors feel the need to strive for such deep self-awareness:

> One thing I keep thinking about when you guys are talking is I hear two goals. One is to be an actor—to be a professional—like in any job, and you want to be good at it. Which means the other people who are receiving your service think it's good. It seems to me there are plenty of people who can be good without seeking truth or struggle with self-awareness. "I know myself well" and you may think you probably don't need any of that. You might just be gifted in this one way. To be able to express things but know very little about yourself. That's possible. The other goal is to be self-actualized. You go into acting because you want to be able to not only make a living but to use this as a vehicle for understanding yourself, understanding your anatomy.

Moser's points are quite interesting related to the exploration process. He suggests leaving it up to the individual to explore the motivation or lack of motivation for such study. But Hopwood speculates, "Going back to Jason's example, if the person says 'My goal is to just perform well, and I don't want to know myself at all,' that's okay, but I wonder if that's going to make a whole actor in the end." Furthermore, do you currently have the self-awareness to make that decision? Is a roadblock preventing you from examination? Are you completely satisfied with your present work? Is your approach to acting devoid of a psychology base?

If you seek to enhance your work using the guidelines this book provides, you may wish to address your current roadblock. But be warned, roadblocks can be tricky. And they can sometimes reveal themselves in subtle ways. The moment you call for a line in a scene that you knew backwards and forwards may be the insinuation of a roadblock. You may have called for a line because your scene partner threw you a new look and you were taken aback by this moment of unplanned interaction on stage. Or perhaps you called for the line because of a lack of specificity and analysis leading to muddy choices and your desire to "keep things fresh." It may mean that this is the part of the scene you dread because of the emotional content. All hint at larger possible issues. Calling for a line is just one of many possible small clues you may be overlooking.

You may want to record and watch your work for signs of a barrier. A personal, dispassionate viewing of a recording of your work may reveal moments when a roadblock creates obstructions to good acting. It must be noted that, for some, watching their work can actually compound their roadblocks because of their harsh self-critique. Moser notes, "In some cases, video playback could backfire because this reflexive self-feedback could lead to obsession rather than objectivity." Others enjoy the experience as it reveals moments when the roadblock dissipates. Most importantly, watching yourself in performance can reveal your habitual safety behaviors.

## What Are Safety Behaviors?

Safety behaviors are the most easily recognizable manifestations of a roadblock. It is when the roadblock makes a public appearance. A safety behavior is a temporary solution to an anxiety-inducing situation. Since they are on display and repeated, actors might call these habits, tics, or tricks; the actor who avoids eye contact during especially intimate moments on stage, or the young actor who keeps tugging at his clothing because he is insecure with his body. More often than not, safety behaviors creep into your acting based on your roadblock. You use them to distract others or keep yourself feeling safe, when in actuality, they make your roadblock even more obvious. Further information related to safety behaviors can be found in the research of social phobias by David M. Clark and Adrian Wells.

In rehearsal for a production I directed, I worked with an actor who constantly put her hand to her mouth at moments of high stress in the play. I had the assistant director count the number of times she did so. It was scores of times in one rehearsal. I made the actor aware of this safety behavior, and the next day she transferred that tension to biting her lip. The assistant director counted again: scores of times. I made the actor aware of how the safety behavior had moved. The next day, the actor played with her hair too many times to count. Later, the actress admitted that all of these minor safety behaviors added up to the fact that she was scared about going to the emotionally vulnerable territory required for the show. Sometimes, the safety behavior can be literal symbols of anxiety, such as covering the mouth and biting the lip, subconsciously trying to avoid the lines for which she was emotionally unprepared. They can also be distractions, like playing with the hair, that keep the actor focused on something other than the high stakes.

What are your habitual manifestations of tension in your personal self in relation to your character? These habits can be related to your roadblock, such as the physical parts of your body that ache at the end of the day or following performance because of where you carry tension. You may discover the many characters you play also carry tension in a similar fashion. You may find that in everyday life, you keep your voice too quiet and too timid for people to hear. Similarly, your characters have the same vocal issue. Once identified, safety behaviors can be eliminated. As choreologist Dr. Katia Savrami notes in her article "Does Dance Matter? The Relevance of Dance Technique in Professional Actor Training": "[actors] should also free their body from movement habits, which are accumulated while living, in order to achieve the physical transformation of moods and ideas and embody the character. The physical presence of the actor/actress on stage requires an 'extraordinary' body."

A complete catalog of your physical habits is required. This is carried out so safety behaviors may be eliminated. More often, like in the example of the actor covering her mouth, the tics simply move to a new place until they are discovered anew, revealing that a physical impairment to good acting can indeed be psychologically based.

Roadblocks and safety behaviors can sometimes be falsely diagnosed as merely vocal and physical impediments. In this case, you may simply need more skill training. Unless these barriers are congenital, they may point to a physical or vocal symptom or safety behavior (as shown in the examples above) that reveals deeper internal issues. So, while you may consistently receive notes related to physical and vocal adjustments, your larger issue may be related to the roadblock that causes the physical tension in performance or quiets your voice from being heard.

An interesting exchange occurred in class between Hopwood and a student related to these safety behaviors, physical "tells" (like an obvious reaction when playing poker), or triggers:

**Student:** If you have a physical safety behavior, for me as an actor, it's not the director's job to continue to call me on my triggers, so what steps can I take to (a) find those triggers, and (b) neutralize them?

**Hopwood:** First you have to identify what those safety behaviors are, and certainly find somebody who can help you because you are not going to necessarily know. You can record your work or you can do a fly-on-the-wall observation of yourself acting. And if you have some sort of tic, or cue or tell, where you noticed that at that exact moment, "Oh I was not feeling well or comfortable," and you begin to notice it at similar times. Once that happens, you will want to get rid of it, but the intermediary step is reflecting on it, so that you know it's happening. That's why I feel people have a hard time with this. For example, I had an issue where I would curl my toes at moments of high stress. I didn't know this until my therapist pointed it out, and she can't see my toes but knew something was up, and she would say, "Scan your body, what are you doing?" and I noticed that my toes would curl, and she said, "Do you notice that every time we get to [this subject] your toes curl up?" So when I noticed my toes curling up, it told me that something was making me anxious. I had to stop and reflect on what was happening around me that was making my toes curl up.

Hopwood advocates for the examination of safety behaviors to allow you to again be intimately aware of your acting process. The other strategy he mentioned includes a self-observation technique often called "fly on the wall" developed by Ayduk and Kross. This is a way to examine situations from a removed, rational perspective to avoid ruminating over an issue—in our case, safety behaviors. So in stressful situations, you would "remove" yourself and think like an outside person (or fly on the wall) observing the stressful situation. No matter the technique, by taking stock of everything internally and externally, and taking responsibility for what safety behaviors you find, you gain a broader knowledge of your three selves. It allows you the ability to write a roadblock statement.

## What Is a Roadblock Statement?

A roadblock statement is a self-reflexive sentence that incorporates all the information provided in the Chapters 2 and 3 and summarizes an impediment in your work. It informs, in broad generalizations, your current work and how a roadblock may manifest itself. The statement usually has a cause and an effect.

Before you create your personal roadblock statement, you have another exercise to complete. In Exercise 4.1 you are asked to write down the strengths of your work and the areas of struggle. The first column is for all your strengths (your comedic timing, your energy, and your ability to craft intricately hilarious stage business), while the second is for all your struggles within your craft (your inability to take a scene seriously, your lack of honesty in darker material, and your fear of connecting on stage).

## Exercise 4.1 Write down a list of qualities about your work as an actor in two columns

From that list, you have the beginnings of your roadblock statement. Those strengths and weaknesses, which have been shaped and deepened by the assessments in this chapter and the exercises related to your craft in Chapter 2, should allow you to create a self-aware and honest declaration of what you think you need to address related to your acting. In order to offer clarity, a roadblock statement should be simple and succinct.

Three possible roadblock statements for the actor who is dissatisfied with only doing comedy might be:

(1) judges his work because he lacks the experience to truly understand the needs of the dramatic actor while on stage.

OR

(2) is uncomfortable with dramatic work so he turns serious moments into jokes in performance.

OR

(3) relies on humor to avoid intimacy on stage.

The statement holds the key to how to best address your work. Based on the dissatisfaction expressed by the actor, the first roadblock statement seems a bit too pat and not nearly as honest or introspective as it could be. Any accountability for the actor's contribution to the roadblock is blamed on lack of opportunity when, in reality, those opportunities to explore dramatic work have presented themselves. Novello opines, "My own view is that the roadblock is likely to be outside a person's initial awareness. So you could say something general like, 'I'm a fairly extroverted person, so being a really shy character might be hard for me.' But that's a little bit superficial, isn't it? It's not clear what's leading the person to be shy." Novello calls for deeper examination.

The second statement is closer to taking ownership of the roadblock but does not address the motivation for the statement. Why does he make jokes in dramatic moments? The third statement comes closest to an introspective, understandable, and reasonable roadblock statement. The issue is clearly an impediment to the kind of acting the actor expressed he wanted to do.

Using the list from the previous exercise as a springboard, begin to craft your roadblock statement (Exercise 4.2). Remember to write in the third person. Do not write it if it is not true. Revise it until you believe you have delved to the heart of the matter. Do you believe this to be true about your acting? Also make sure to add the caveat "while acting" or "on stage" or something similar to remind you that this is work on your professional self.

## Exercise 4.2   Write a roadblock statement

Examine the statement and its implications for your work. Examine it in relation to the résumé exercise (2.6) and see if the statement rings true. Examine it in relation to your varied assessment data and see if they align. More than likely, this initial statement is just the beginning of a long journey to eradicating those unwanted limitations in your work.

What follows are some examples of roadblock statements written by actors participating in the studio classes focused on this subject:

— *uses quietness and subtlety to avoid how outlandish a character needs to be on stage.*

— *relies on humor and transformation to avoid looking stupid or boring as himself on stage.*

— *overanalyzes her choices to the point that she sometimes doesn't make one or dilutes and censors it until it's too small to recognize on stage.*

— *avoids certain aspects of her characters and hides behind their seriousness to avoid looking foolish as actor.*

— *plays being innocent to avoid being sexual as actor.*

— *uses her familiarity with her ballet training as a way to avoid being present in the moment to calm her anxiety as an actor.*

— *hides behind scholarly work and analysis to avoid addressing other parts of her acting.*

— *avoids the negative aspects of a character to prevent being seen as imperfect or flawed on stage.*

*— avoids making large choices to ensure she doesn't make the wrong ones as actor.*

*— uses authority to avoid exposing personal weak spots as actor.*

*— plays it small to avoid taking up space as an actor.*

*— "decides" for the character rather than allowing other options to emerge— because he's afraid of living in power and strength while acting.*

Lest you only focus on the negative aspects or boundaries in your work, this statement can also expose your assets as an actor that should be lauded and respected. Hopwood notes, "Finding out where those weaknesses are, where you were not strong, also reveals where your strength lies, where you are strong. And by trying to attack those places where you need to work, it also reinforces the work that you already have ownership of."

If you are that actor who hides behind comedy in order to avoid revealing real vulnerability on stage, you are also a great comedic actor. If your need for perfection gets in the way of your sense of play on stage, you are also a highly technical actor. If you hide behind your intelligence in order to appear looking foolish on camera, you are a smart actor. Hopwood sees the merits: "So you remain fulfilled in the places that you are already good with." The inverse can mollify any fears about the impending work on your current roadblock.

In Exercise 4.3, you will write an inverse of the roadblock statement. Write it in the third person again, and make sure you give yourself the credit you deserve, making sure you understand that the mechanisms you create to succeed as an actor are also good things.

## Exercise 4.3    Create an inverse sentence of the roadblock statement

What follows are the same examples from earlier with their inverse statements:

*— uses quietness and subtlety to avoid how outlandish a character needs to be.*

*— can use quietness and subtlety to share intimate moments with an audience.*

*— relies on humor and transformation to avoid looking stupid or boring as himself on stage.*

*— feels comfortable making BIG CHOICES on stage!*

— *overanalyzes her choices to the point that she sometimes doesn't make one or dilutes and censors it until it's too small to recognize on stage.*
— *choices make sense with the given circumstances that are thought-out when acting.*

— *avoids certain aspects of her characters and hides behind their seriousness to avoid looking foolish as actor.*
— *is able to bring less obvious aspects of her characters to the fore in performance.*

— *plays being innocent to avoid being sexual as actor.*
— *can play younger roles.*

— *uses her familiarity with her ballet training as a way to avoid being present in the moment to calm her anxiety as an actor.*
— *has the discipline that comes with her training that allows her to channel that strength and transform it into commanding a strong stage presence.*

— *hides behind scholarly work and analysis to avoid addressing other parts of her acting.*
— *characters have depth and power on stage.*

— *avoids the negative aspects of a character to prevent being seen as imperfect or flawed.*
— *is always able to charm the audience.*

— *avoids making large choices to ensure she doesn't make the wrong ones as actor.*
— *is a calculated and well thought-out actor.*

— *uses authority to avoid exposing personal weak spots as actor.*
— *has strong drive in her scenes.*

— *plays it small to avoid taking up space as an actor.*
— *creates deep internal connections with the characters that she brings to life.*

— *"decides" for the character rather than allowing other options to emerge— because he's afraid of living in power and strength while acting.*
— *has ready access to his vulnerability while acting.*

## What Do I Do With My Roadblock Statement?

The roadblock statement is yours to do with as you wish. You may find that simply writing the statement lessens the power of the roadblock in your work. It can also diminish over time by simply acknowledging its presence. For a few, the roadblock is too overwhelming a task to deal with currently. The work can begin at a later date, when time, emotion, and focus seem a better match. But for most, the power of the roadblock statement leads you to start making some connections to work that has lacked the requisite freedom or an emotional heft in the past. The roadblock statement is something to concentrate on during script analysis, auditions, performance, and between gigs. You can begin the journey to creating a bridge to the work you want to achieve.

Marika Reisberg says that creating the roadblock statement is like "an onion and you go at it in layers. In movement terms, it allows someone to drop deeper. It's difficult because you get mixed signals. If I am 'a perfectionist who doesn't want to disappoint anyone' by identifying perfectionism the perception is I am already letting someone down. I also get positive reinforcement for being prepared." The mixed signals offer a conundrum for an actor working on roadblocks. If the actor in the example has relied on his humor and it has gotten him work, what will he be left with?

Humor will not leave the actor and can be summoned at any time. This introspection calls for openness to the process, as Reisberg notes, "This could set you up for rigidness, unless you have a beginner's mind that allows you to look at the roadblock in new and surprising ways and making a choice to change the pattern if that is something you have value in." If the actor in the example is seeking a broader range of dramatic work, then most likely he sees the value in the process. But Reisberg continues that he must look deeper: "Exploring beneath this pattern is necessary. What reminds you of this pattern and when is it retriggered in your work? Embody the pattern. How does it physically move in your body? The removal of all of these layers can unlock subconscious material."

The subconscious is a powerful friend to the roadblock statement and usually points to a deeper pattern of unresolved or unexplored issues that may intersect the three selves—personal, professional, and character. In acting classes, it is only the purview of the latter two that is territory to explore. But by addressing this pattern in your work life, there may be personal crossover that must be monitored and examined (solely by the actor) throughout the process in order to maintain a healthy approach to perfecting your craft. So for example, "— uses physical and vocal tricks to avoid sharing his true self on stage" may hint at larger issues in his personal self. He has wisely identified his safety behaviors as actor (for example, physical and vocal pyrotechnics that camouflage his work). He really only needs to concentrate on the last section which proclaims, he does not share his true self on stage. Now, if he wants to explore what prevents him from doing that off stage, that is personal work. In acting class, the questions should surround the work: "Is it is a fear of judgment that guides his choices professionally?"; "Is it a lack of belief in his own talents that prevent him from his best work?"; "Is his work overshadowed by his constant need to please others?" By focusing the questions on the professional self, there is clearer delineation of where the work needs to be done.

The most common root of the roadblock for the actor is most likely found in relation to the following issues: anxiety, body awareness, fear of emotion, disproportionate extrovert/introvert tendencies, physical or emotional hiding, inability to achieve intimacy, self-judgment, need for or fear of power, low self-esteem, inability to trust, and, the most common, a lack of vulnerability. Vulnerability, as well as anxiety, intersects with all of the issues mentioned, and they all have smaller, interesting connections to each other in some way. Since each actor's journey and roadblock is specific and individual, your issue may not be included here, or it may be a combination of two or more of the issues mentioned. These issues, which most commonly affect the actor self and yet are deeply rooted in the personal self, are examined in Chapter 7 of this book. More specifics related to how a roadblock manifests itself in the actor, advice from the consultants, questions for the actor, and sources for supplemental reading are included there as well.

The identification of this roadblock in your work as an actor must also be examined in your characters. Do all of your characters have a similar roadblock? Is your professional roadblock also limiting all the characters you create? Is this roadblock something that impedes your work? If so, are you willing to address it?

Understanding the combination and interlacing of the three levels of self is important. So, while you may be aware that you are a cautious person when it comes to trust in your personal life, you understand that an actor must have some level of trust (in partner, director, or the process) when plying your chosen trade. You also may be playing a character that, through your analysis, is completely innocent and trusts others unconditionally. How can these facts, colored by your issues with trust, work together to create a symbiosis of selves? Through a keen awareness of the roadblock, careful self-examination, and goals set across the three selves, an actor who has personal trust issues may create a character who is entirely trusting. As an example, set a goal for your personal self to mingle with the cast during breaks of rehearsal rather than your normal pattern of checking your phone to distract from interaction. For the professional self, use "trust" as the basis of your script analysis and make choices that require trust in your scene partner. And for your character self, set the goal of openness in creating a character who deeply trusts those around her. This attention to the roadblock and its connection to the three selves can be entirely productive. However, it can also make you hyper-aware and obsessive of each choice you make, especially if you do not succeed immediately. That sort of obsession can negatively impact an actor. As is revealed in the following study, an actor's psychological wellbeing can affect their performance and cause professional anxiety, no matter the geographical or methodological approach to acting.

Ian Maxwell, Dr. Mark Seton, and Dr. Marianna Szabó worked with the Australian Equity Foundation (a branch of the Australian Actors' Equity) to create a groundbreaking study on the health and wellbeing practices of actors. With access to a large pool of actors, the survey sought information related to things such as alcohol and drug use, job satisfaction, and preparation for the financial worries specifically related to the profession of acting. The results are eye-opening for both actors and actor educators.

"The Australian Actors' Wellbeing Study" examined two important elements related to the topic of this book. First, the study looked at work-related health complaints of actors and found that the majority of actors identified physical woes as their major concern related to the profession, followed closely by psychological complaints. Vocal complaints fell lower on the survey. This alarmingly high percentage of psychological, health-related complaints affecting performance demands attention as seen in Table 4.1.

Another key finding is that nearly 40 percent of actors agreed that they had trouble "letting go" after performing a particularly demanding role.

**Table 4.1   The nature of performance-affecting health-related complaints (adapted from "The Australian Actors' Wellbeing Study," see Maxwell, Seton, and Szabó, 2015)**

The nature of performance affecting health-related complaint (percentage for those reporting a complaint

| | | |
|---|---|---|
| Mainly vocal | 72 | 19.8% |
| Mainly bodily | 118 | 32.5% |
| Mainly psychological | 89 | 24.5% |
| Overall complaint | 84 | 23.1% |

These findings confirm what this book espouses, the need for a clearer separation of self and character. These findings (Table 4.2) also incite advocacy for assistance to actors, which currently falls outside most theatrical training and theatrical actor services (like unions).

The study concurs and calls for the inclusion of psychological wellbeing and maintenance in curriculum for actor training programs. It suggests more attention to regularized cooling down or decompression exercises for post-performance work (covered in Chapter 9.) This study is excellent evidence that current methods of education must begin to carefully tread into the psychological wellbeing of actors when training them. It also challenges the notion of emotion-based acting as a purely American approach.

Mark Seton also continues this excellent work on the personal wellbeing of actors through webinars, workshops, and writings. His fascinating approach to "resilient vulnerability"™ is a great source for expanded education on topics raised within this book. His approach

**Table 4.2   Letting go after performance (adapted from "The Australian Actors' Wellbeing Study," see Maxwell, Seton, and Szabó, 2015)**

Have you experienced any difficulties in relaxing or "letting go" after performing an emotionally and physically demanding role?

| | | |
|---|---|---|
| Yes | 303 | 38.7% |
| No | 324 | 41.4% |
| No response | 171 | 21.9% |

serves as a model for the type of actor education this book advocates and the study suggests.

The primary focus of roadblock work is on your craft, but it can also negatively impact your personal self. Dr. Moser was visiting a class when a student asked about the mixing of personal issues and professional work:

**Student:** Say that you are working on something in your acting that hits a nerve personally, and you know it's triggering some deeply rooted psychological issues that you have. How do you get past that?

**Moser:** How stuck it is or how deeply rooted it is will probably determine how much time it will take to deal with that. You want to keep a separation of personal and professional, at some level anyway. Maybe you want to see a value to be as vulnerable as you can be as a person, as well as be as vulnerable as you can as a professional, but those don't have to be exactly the same; you can start making choices about whether you want to address a deeply rooted nerve or not [personally or professionally]. So I think a lot of it starts with making a choice about whether this is something that hits a nerve for you. If you don't want it to hit that nerve anymore, you don't have to.

The idea of choice is key in Moser's response, but if your choice is to more deeply examine your craft and personal issues, to overtake that journey, you may need to seek assistance outside of the studio with others more qualified to handle your concerns. As mentioned throughout the book, self-examination takes many forms, and if this unavoidable linkage between professional and personal self becomes overwhelming, personal health wins every time.

## What Can I Do?

It is important to objectively examine all the information you gleaned from the assessments. The actor's craft is full of ego and defense. Understandably, actors depend upon their personal interpretative, emotional, and empathic skills in order to be successful in their profession. It is therefore with some apprehension that actors begin to examine what can be perceived as a shortcoming. Just as any businessperson with ambition must target her limitations and strategize to best overcome them, so must you thoughtfully examine yours. But unlike the businessperson who must address time management, meeting deadlines, and interpersonal communication, the actor must do a holistic examination of professional, self, and character.

One common area where an actor's defense may impede your work is the receiving of criticism. An actor working on a roadblock is highly focused on the roadblock and its suppression. In these instances, you can misinterpret or mishear valuable feedback because of your sensitivity and focus on the issue at hand. Having feedback so targeted on one issue, as opposed to the general notes you normally receive, can leave an actor flummoxed.

One school of thought that has been helpful is the message of Acceptance Commitment Theory (with the ironic acronym, ACT). This theory is about compassionate, non-judgmental awareness, and it is a tangible way in which actors may begin to examine their work more objectively. The basic precept of this philosophy is akin to mindfulness (explored in Chapter 9). ACT pragmatically asks that you become aware of the issue, accept that it is only current, and embrace it as a part of who you are at this moment. Rather than dwell on the fact that you are presently limited in one aspect of your acting, it reminds you that this is only a temporary state of being. Moser concurs, "Absolutely, there is a level of acceptance. Accepting this is what you are going to be good at, but you are not going to be good at it this time because of a professional issue—that roadblock or personal issue. That roadblock is going to change; it's going to lessen over time."

Acceptance that you are somehow limiting yourself can be also empowering. It creates clear and tangible goals. Rather than the generalized success you aimed for in the past, your work now has a target. Moser warns, "I like to think that we have boundless potential, so we can all unlock potential, somewhere in there, there are no limits to anybody. But as things typically play out, even if we have this potential that we can unlock, most of us don't unlock it, or some of us don't unlock it fully, even before we are dead. That's just the reality of things." Despite the nihilistic tone, Moser does offer some hope: "You can succeed with an acceptance of where you are currently and what things you aren't immediately going to get past." Unlocking the potential he describes may result in access to a fleet of emotions currently unused, but, for now, acceptance of your current situation is key.

Work on your roadblock is your decision, but obsessing over the problem offers no comfort and, most likely, those negative thoughts give power to the issue. So, remaining aware but not concerned about your current roadblock will offer a much healthier and happier journey to freedom in your acting. Allow yourself space, time, freedom, and acceptance as you work on your craft. You can also occasionally or temporarily set aside the work when it becomes overwhelming. You can approach the roadblock when you are ready.

## What Is the Role of the Teacher?

For the most part, the teacher has been conspicuously absent from this very private and personal exploration for the actor. But it is at this moment that the acting teacher or director can assist. The following chapters explore how the teacher and student can work in concert to address the roadblock. But with the teacher as guide in such personal territory, there can sometimes be a crossover into some tricky ethical questions.

Hopwood elaborates: "I would question the word 'sometimes.' I think that it's inevitable, and I think that's why this is a complicated job for you, Rob, because it's hard to imagine someone's acting roadblock not being very similar to their personal roadblock. So you were right; you have to be careful not to go too far into personal matters because that's not what we're here for."

Ironically, after a visit to my graduate acting class where he spent time answering questions from the actors, I received the following in an email from Hopwood: "I was a little worried when we got to [a student's] issue that I went a little too far. That is the line that we keep discussing, but I found myself kind of twisting and hedging and getting a little discombobulated to try to stay on topic and get back to acting (just acting!)."

The fascinating examination of boundaries between student and teacher permeated a lot of my time with the consultants. As covered earlier in the "A Note to Acting Teachers" introductory section, the unique convergence of personal and professional openness necessary to educate actors forces you as teacher or director to consider your boundaries daily with regard to the examination of the human condition. Hopwood spoke with me about the similarity to his work in psychology:

I want to be close with my supervisees but I'm not their therapist, and I'm not trying to change their personalities. Although learning how to do therapy, much like learning acting, probably does change your personality in some ways. So, I don't know; it's very gray, and you know you're crossing a boundary when it's happening, but it's pretty hard to see ahead of time, and then once you're there, it's hard to know what to do about it other than to say "I think maybe we just went too far, maybe let's go back." I mean, we are both constantly faced with this issue of, "Did we get too personal or go too far?" So you want to be available and to help them understand how that might relate to their job, but at the same time, you want to maintain the professional roles. That seems like the basic challenge for the job.

In this very personal work, there is also an element that students are perhaps willing to risk or share more with the hope of pleasing the educator rather than of successfully completing the homework. The focus should be on the ultimate goal of freedom in acting—not on the assignment. Novello worries, "There's an expectation—I mean it's a class right. There's a performance element. I have to impress my teacher and that is by being vulnerable and being exposed and then that is the test—I'm wondering how much of this might get in the way of one's ability to be able to truly address the roadblock." Reisberg expands the debate: "I guess I would be curious too—what is the acting culture in the room? There is this culture that you're going to do what your director or professor asks you to do. And then if you find if you really dig deep, do I get a better score or am I doing better? As opposed to focusing on the work."

Even if the culture in your acting studio forgoes deep, emotional connection, it must be clear that students can put barriers, limitations, and restrictions on their own work. As you design the safe space for any deep acting work, the questions raised about boundaries and the culture of the studio are excellent thoughts for you to have in the fore-front of coaching acting. Creating a healthy studio can be provided by setting limits, giving clear guidance, and paying careful attention to coaching, all leading to the moment when you will assist actors to build a bridge in their work. I am not implying that each day you enter the classroom you aren't hoping to assist an actor to a personal epiph-any, but the personal boundaries of roadblocks may be a need for more regulation. Each day in the studio is a struggle to connect concepts and manage the growth of dozens of actors, but this sort of systematized and/or group exploration of roadblocks calls for careful guidance.

I have seen studios where a teacher recoils from making adjustments for fear that it will stunt an actor's growth, when, in actuality, that practice simply reinforces bad habits and safety behaviors. I have seen educators at the other extreme, where students appear to be "risking" in their work when all they are doing is making the choices the educator prescribed for them. Learning habits are different for each student and creative freedom is achieved through various ways. Observation about what clicks for a certain student and leaves others cold should be noted. Interviews with students about the way they like to learn is encouraged. Understanding roadblocks and knowing when students are hiding behind them is also important. Knowing when to confront those roadblocks and when to leave them alone is the ultimate key to this work in the classroom.

One of the actors in my studio class had the roadblock that he relied on being the nice guy and using all his readily available vulnerability to charm the audience. Even after identifying that roadblock, he analyzed Trigorin from Anton Chekhov's *The Seagull* as a misunderstood gentle man who deeply loved Nina. While this may be a fine approach for someone needing to work on those issues, this student's roadblock-filtered reading of the script related to the character's actions and what other characters say about Trigorin showed a lack of connection between roadblock and analysis. I felt perfectly within my rights to force his choices to darker places.

The most difficult area to traverse is the personal boundaries of educator and student. I do not imply that, as educator, there is ever any right time to use personal information to spur on deeper acting. I also recognize that actors and educators are constantly required by the text to create characters with questionable values or explore dramatic territory that pushes accepted societal boundaries. Negotiating such territory must be handled with caution and respect by both parties. Actors and educators want to expand restrictions in order to create work that is absent of roadblocks. This is a primary goal for all. Unfortunately, some educators use such boundary-pushing work to actually cross them. Crossing boundaries includes using personal information of the students' lives, bringing up unhealthy emotional suppositions based on your personal knowledge of the student, and guiding them to emotional territory without having strategies to assist them in returning from such places. These and other tactics are to be avoided. If you fear that boundaries are being crossed rather than pushed, it is best to pull yourself back.

# 5    Roadblock Examples

What follows in this chapter are real examples from actors writing about their roadblocks and their experiences in reducing them. I chose various responses from professional, undergraduate, graduate, male, and female actors over a broad range of ages who were all affected by some of the most common roadblocks. By reading about their experiences, you may better understand your personal roadblock. You will note the strategies they used (many of which will appear in Chapter 6) and experiment with adopting or adapting them for yourself. Throughout the examples, you will see the thoughtful approach that this work demands. In some cases, you will also read about the crossover of the roadblock into personal matters. This debate throughout these testimonials may give you a clearer possible definition of how the three selves intersect for you. You will also read examples in which the roadblock may appear throughout performance work, from auditions through closing night. Roadblocks expose themselves in different ways, depending on the unique demands of different genres and mediums. Because roadblocks can make appearances everywhere, examples are offered from musical theater, comedy, film, and other styles.

## What Have Other Actors Experienced?

Here are a few roadblock statements and testimonials from actors who have shared their experiences in order to assist with the overcoming of your obstacles.

"— uses speed to push past truly emotional moments while acting."
*My roadblock statement came from a number of issues from different areas. I was not aware that I used speed to avoid things that made me uncomfortable on stage (and in life). But I did know that being in social situations always made me talk too fast, stutter, blush, and say things I didn't want to say; and that during rehearsal, I was ALWAYS given the note to go slower, to spend more time in my words, and to do less. With help, I've*

*traced this back to my avoidance of highly emotional situations. This, in a very personal way, connects to my home life, and the emotional temperature growing up. But, when I first started working on becoming more open to emotion and honest response, I had no idea that these areas were linked.*

*While working on roadblocks, I started to organize my thoughts before each show. I decided to concentrate on one or two words for each performance. The words were verbs that I could use for different people in the cast: degrade, diminish, lift, protect, etc., basic Acting 101 stuff—find your objective and work for it. But finding new words every night brought out different elements of the story, and I found it really helpful to keep working on being vulnerable and alive. As I've mentioned, having emotion has been something I've understood to be very negative, silly, or dumb my whole life. This time last year, I would not have been able to begin to navigate this emotional territory. In class, I was given a scene that directly related to my speed issue, and the first time I took a pass at the scene, I felt like I had the correct inner life, but it wasn't coming out. The next couple of times I tried it, it felt like trying on a new body. I kept falling out of it and moving like me then catching myself, but I started to do it as the character, not myself. The feeling I had while I was working on the scene was kind of like being at the back of a tunnel, or stepping back from a picture. I was putting something else first and it felt crazy. I loved it. It was so out there, reckless, wild, free, and uncontrollable. I could not do these things the year before because of my negative association with high emotion, mood swings, irrational behavior, or spontaneity. It took a long time to be able to identify, manage, and change my habits that I used to avoid serious feelings in my life and on stage. I tried many things that worked for me: autodrama, vulnerability exercises, releasing the need to be right/correct, finding new ways to work in rehearsal and in performance, and rerouting my choices through the character. I'm still working all the time on identifying, stopping, and rerouting my choices and mannerisms. It can be really frustrating, and sometimes it feels like I haven't made any progress, but the breadth and depth of the characters I can understand has grown, and taking stock of that has been rewarding. I feel good about the progress I've made and am really looking forward to the future.*

"— uses her intelligence to avoid empathy as actor."

*... The "as actor" caveat* [in the roadblock statement] *is a good reminder that these are roadblocks that we are tackling in our study of acting, not necessarily in our personal lives. So while some connect to our*

*personal self, the openness and rawness is only needed on stage. The rest is our own business. It's frustrating that as a pretty wildly empathetic person who can tear up at the mention of anyone else's pain, I could not tap into that empathy on stage. It was walled up. And I have a "tell," with my cheeks turning red and my skin flushing, so when it's real, I know. And I can't fake it. I can't pretend to feel empathy. And when I'm feeling it, there is no hiding it, even if I want to. What's exciting is the sense that I was able to break through that block and experiment with riding out an uncontrolled, unfiltered, unanalyzed emotion. It was a release. My breakthrough arrived in a wave of frustration. A frustration when I thought I had done something right and not overanalyzed the scene, only to be told that the character lacked analysis and too many things were missing from the given circumstance. The frustration came when I tried to ask about the disconnection and instead, I couldn't hold back the tears; that was what ultimately brought on the breaking down of the roadblock. Frustration. What was awesome about that moment was that I never lost control of it. I was in complete control of something that, for the character, could then spiral and spin into chaos. I was able to listen and respond to side-coaching, while still living in that place. And once the moment of the scene was over, the emotional vulnerability was over too. I was a raw actor, not a raw person, and for the first time, that separation was clear. For me, the moment of breakthrough didn't come from sense memory or character backstory or given circumstances. It came from real, in the moment, immediate frustration. But what was ultimately so exciting about that was, the character I was playing felt the same frustration. It was easily transferrable.*

*One of the residual effects of this experience, however, was that the release came in a kind of wave that felt like it was always waiting to happen. That might be the newness of the sensation. But immediately following, and now still several weeks after, it's always there and bubbling right under the surface, ready to fire at any moment. I realized that understanding, confronting, and investigating these roadblocks wasn't a checklist to complete, but was rather an iceberg, the top of which I have only just reached. Once one roadblock is reached, what do I move onto next? What do I tackle and what do I try to overcome? What comforts me about this process is the knowledge that there is no deadline for reaching it, and the end goal is simply to keep working within a creative sphere of self-awareness that allows me to explore. And "end goal" isn't even the right word because, ideally, there is no end. The struggle now is to figure out how to make those moments of connection less random—sustained and always accessible. I'm not sure, but for me, I think it's a sense of slowing down and allowing multiple and different emotions to wash through. To take time to think as the character rather than to insist that, as a smart actor, I already know. To not overcomplicate the matter, when the simplicity is much more honest. It's a "less is more" cliché that reminds me to not try so hard to make characters "be" a certain way, especially if that way always ends up being just another version of me. Studying these roadblocks made me realize how fun it is to find the ways that characters are different than I am so that I can explore and live inside those differences. There is a freedom and flexibility in that, and a way to expand what you have access to in terms of characters. Breaking down the walls that block access to emotions because they also block access to characters, limiting my own type. And it's fun! It's fun to play with losing control when you know it is safe and you will come back. Nothing to be afraid of.*

"— plays 'the victim' because he lacks trust in himself and his partners as actor."

*After we addressed our roadblocks and got it all out on the table, things began to take on a change. I think many of the things about me as an actor are also exactly applicable to me as a person. I don't think the two are separate. You can put a character on, but everything you do as them is filtered through you as you. I'm afraid of criticism and rejection as a person, and so I'm timid, I don't push my agenda, I'm passive, I'm a people pleaser. All of these things translate on stage, when I don't really want control. I would rather follow my scene partner than lead; I want to play the good guy, the nice guy, the hero, the victim. However, just knowing about these roadblocks and confessing them and confronting them is a step in the right direction. On the flip side, I was described as being a good role model, being a good partner, being genuine, thoughtful, hardworking, intuitive, and relatable. These things are great as an actor, but they too come from who I am as a person.*

*The biggest revelation for me in this class was the targeted improv. Before that, I had not realized how quickly I put my characters and myself in the defenseless/victim role. My assignment was to be the aggressor, and I immediately turned it into a "Why did you do to this to me?" every single time we started over. It took me about ten tries before I even realized this, and on top of that, someone else had to say it. And what hit hardest was that, in the moment, I couldn't think in a different way. Victim was my go-to, and I don't possess strong enough abilities to trust myself in the moment. Without that trust, I didn't know what to do, and therefore didn't know what to say, so the scene stalled several times. Once I was onto something emotionally, but then I stalled again. During the rest of class, as I watched the others and thought about my scenes, I was able to come up with a completely different way that I would have approached it. This points out a distinct part of my process. I need to have time to think. I have to own it now. I am someone who sits and analyzes and thinks. I will take in and absorb all the notes I'm given, I will go away and process them, then I will come back with something new and different. But in the moment, without that time to think, I censor and judge and stall. That's a really important take-away. This is how I work. And I need to communicate that to directors. There is a whole new area of openness, trying to get there, trying to remain there so that I can go with my scene partner, let my walls down, and let them in. There is simplicity in my most recent work. A state of being without tension. I'm excited to move forward in my work having had this experience.*

"— diminishes her height so she doesn't inconvenience others when acting."

*What is a roadblock? Literally it is something that blocks the road. It is also a descriptive metaphor for what is blocking the actor from being able to grow. It is what is keeping the actor in their comfort zone. It is the myriad of things that keep the actor from making different choices and develop characters they have never played before. After our self-critique, we were asked to write a roadblock statement for our acting journey to this point. Looking over my self-critique, I asked myself, "Why do you feel this way about yourself? Can you identify an event that made you feel this way?" I noticed a trend. Many of these things were connected with a thought of being an inconvenience to others, hiding myself, or a desire to be small. I should point out now that I am a 6' 1" woman, and I am constantly reminded that I am so tall. Thinking about my time on stage and my daily life, where I was put in the last row, where students complained because they couldn't see over me, people whispering in the audience, "Mommy, I can't see past the tall girl." This is true in my slouching, in my hip popping, in the fact that I find every way humanly possible to make myself shorter. However, even with a life of negative events happening, all of which surround the idea of height, I am working my ass off to overcome these roadblocks that have been built up by the words and actions of others. So how do you overcome a roadblock where you feel that you are an inconvenience to others? You own yourself! One of my strengths as an actor is being able to have fun and play. So when I was working with my scene partner, we played! We played both characters at their highest highs, their lowest lows, and everything in between. It was fun! I realized the more fun I allowed myself to have, the easier it was to give over to wanting what the character wants and staying out of my head, thinking that I was in the way, that I was taller than my partner. I had to commit to feeling sexy, to feeling desirable, and to needing someone. Through scene study I connected to this idea, freedom of choices, and I began to play. Through play, I was focused on all the different choices my character had to make; there was no room for my own self-criticism. I saw my roadblock crumbling, little by little. Each of the characters I was asked to embody had a confidence, power, and desperate need of another. I discovered that I could connect to these traits vocally, but the vocal power was not matched in my physical presence. Having a to-do list in my brain is not always a bad thing. It was when I can chip away at my to-do list through play, rather than analytical prowess, that I started to embody the sensuality of these characters, the confidence and vulnerability to take up space and boldly express a need for another.*

*By identifying my height as a roadblock, I feel that I have been able to make a conscious effort to chip away at it and change my point of view. At this time, I do not feel I have demolished the roadblock, but now knowing it exists, and that by allowing it to impact me I have limited the amount of play I can do in the arts, I am more determined than ever to be kind to myself and try my hardest to look all 6' 1" of myself and be appreciative of who I am and what I am capable of by owning my height through conscious effort and dedication.*

"— limits his choices in order to be liked on stage."

*Defining what limits oneself takes bravery. Working on a roadblock is not about beating yourself up. It's about taking control of the wheel. After I wrote [my statement] down on a piece of paper, I thought, "Ah. There it is. Done. Let's move on to something else." I had to remind myself throughout the process to be brave and seek solutions while sharpening the focus of the stumbling block. In doing so, I found that I substitute vulnerability for physicality because I love the quality of sensitivity that I possess.*

*Therefore, my roadblock is directly linked to a desire for being liked and being accepted. That's a perfectly acceptable way of walking through the world, should I so choose to. And by no means is anyone trying to change my identity or persona. But when my roadblock is self-imposed on my work, then the separating thought between character and actor is muddled. I felt trapped in certain choices. I never had the courage to ask why? Until now.*

*Turns out, I've spent a long time imposing my thought onto the character rather than the other way around. Many times, that would work and be successful. But sometimes it wouldn't. Sometimes it would feel flat out wrong. And that was when the logic didn't add up somewhere. The logic of the character must be different than my own. Investigating my roadblock, I discovered that it related to my interpretation of a character, and therefore, was a place for me to hide and make safe and/or repetitive choices. We each have our own perspectives on life, and bringing that to rehearsal is a blessing, not a curse. But getting stuck in certain choices and not being able to read text objectively is a roadblock that will end an actor's growth as a character. We were assigned scenes from Chekhov's* The Seagull. *I was tasked to play Trigorin. I saw him as a dark, brooding writer who struggles mightily with his own work and his view of the world. He has a strong sense of morality. It never even occurred to me that Trigorin could be the exact opposite. My initial read was habitual. Every character I play must be justly good and with the best of intentions. When I play "bad" people, they aren't bad—they just do bad things. It took the moment of being called out by my classmates that I saw the ridiculousness of my initial impulse. Upon further investigation, I found the pseudo-sexual, libido-driven, egomaniacal side of Trigorin that I had never even pondered as a possibility previously. This [knowledge] afforded me the opportunity to discover that my roadblock can be overcome simply by acknowledging it exists and asking it to kindly step aside so I can do my work. In doing so, it was as though I was given an entirely different brush and color to use on my canvas. It is a condition to come back to and revisit when working on any character. Have a clean slate, investigate the character, reread what you thought it was going to be. Choose an opposite approach. Play. Don't decide. Don't protect and guard and look right. Not every character—not any character has to be a certain way. Listen. Respond. Read the play again. Don't decide. The goal is to be another character and to be able to turn him on and off at my own will. I know that conquering one roadblock leads to the next. That will always be the nature of the beast. Because replicating the human condition is tough stuff. The key is not to be overcome by the challenges one faces, but to be driven by them. Having the imagination and the nerve to use it takes bravery.*

"— is afraid of looking foolish as actor so she makes small choices."

*I have come to realize that my roadblock (or, in any case, one of them) has to do with my own fear of looking ridiculous. The very first thing we did was isolate what our roadblock was. I have to admit that my roadblock was there for reasons that I really didn't want to look at too closely; layers upon layers that have built up like the layers of wax on a candle until they coated me, the proverbial wick. If I'm to continue that metaphor, then I suppose that this experience has been a hot light bulb, melting away the wax without burning me up. Nobody wants to blurt out their weaknesses for the entire world to hear, especially not actors. I think actors, in general, really try to separate the personal from the professional, perhaps even more than other, more conventional professions. We have to have such a fine line drawn between who we are as people and who we are as actors because our profession comes with certain inherent risks that the line will blur, and that is something that cannot happen.*

*We did exercises to access our vulnerability, and I don't think I've ever experienced anything quite like them. They inspired an almost physical change in me—one that I felt for the rest of the day. I was, for all intents and purposes, awed by the realization that a simple exercise could inspire that much of a change within myself. It was game-changing. For the first time, I truly realized what vulnerability was—and how much work it was to get into that headspace. I think that the techniques we have been taught and the sort of coaching we have been given have the potential to help a lot of people along their road to better acting. I'm grateful for the experience, and I honestly think that I am a better actor for having done all of it.*

Viewing these responses showcases the wide variety of roadblocks. Also apparent is the focus and difficult work necessary to address individual barriers, while at the same time, several of the testimonials cover how "fun" it is to work in a new way. Throughout, you may have noted the variety of techniques and strategies used by the actors to examine their work, which will be covered in the next chapter. Some strategies were externally based, while the majority required internal adjustments. You may also note that each actor achieved some form of success; this was consistent throughout all the classes devoted to addressing roadblocks. The journey takes time and these actors were willing to commit to both the exploration and the difficult work required for such honest self-analysis.

## How Can Roadblocks Affect the Rehearsal Process?

For any actor, an audition is fraught with high emotion and ultimately determines whether or not you will get to play the role. For most actors, the act of walking into the audition room amplifies the roadblock and the accompanying safety behaviors. The nervous safety behaviors are "necessary" to calm you down (although they have the opposite effect). The physical insecurities appear center stage within you as you stand center stage. The audition is a chance for you to show your best work, but for some actors with roadblocks, it pushes you back to the safe, limited, and expected choices of the past, where neither the casting director nor you are surprised by your audition. The fears and worries so natural at auditions can be lessened by examining and replicating the audition process through planned and calculated rehearsals with minor goals related to each separate event—the entrance, the introduction, the performance (song, monologues, or scene), the follow-up, and the exit. So these small goals might include making eye contact when entering, not displaying safety behaviors during the introduction, exploring vulnerability in the performance, staying open during the follow-up small talk, and walking confidently during the exit. By creating mini-goals for each of these standard events, the actor may reduce the safety behaviors and eventually the roadblock.

## Exercise 5.1   Set goals for an upcoming audition

Early in the reading of a draft of this book, a professional actor friend, Barry Delaney, wrote to me about a roadblock in a recent audition. He writes, "I had a commercial audition yesterday. It was a dad celebrating after his kid gets a word right in a spelling bee. So I [prepared] a dance move, and when I demonstrated for my own kids what I was going to do, it was awesome and hilarious. But I couldn't find that freedom or looseness when I was at the audition. It was okay, but it wasn't as good as it had been." As it does to many, this roadblock revealed itself to him in an audition. When rehearsing, he notes, "I'm my natural self. Unselfconscious. Free." With a focus on roadblocks, he tried to figure out the reason for his restricted audition and the audition process for him in general. He continues, "I couldn't get past caring about how I was being perceived, so I tried to control that. To present myself in a certain way. So I ended up being less true than I am in a room full of kids." His issue is the same for many actors in the audition room, and despite its frequency, actors sometime seem to accept the issue as an integral element of auditioning, rather than a roadblock that can be overcome.

There is also a rare and strange phenomenon that happens to a few actors in the audition related to this highly anxiety-producing event. Because they are already in an altered emotional state, they are sometimes able to access the blocked vulnerable and free work necessary within the actual audition situation. This is because of two factors: the temporary aspect of the visit to this emotional territory that is sustained momentarily and the desperation for the work. These two elements combine with the high emotion to make the audition a unique experience. Following that euphoric, temporary free work, most actors experience a nagging fear that, should they get the part, they will never be able to achieve the unblocked work again. That suspicion alone negatively reinforces the temporary freedom achieved in the audition. There have been experiences where actors were amazing in the audition and then choked in the rehearsal process, but these are few and far between; however, a continual access to such freedom is necessary.

Throughout the rehearsal process, the mingling of the three versions of actors (self, actor, and character) occurs: "I want colleagues to like me personally." "I want them to respect my work ethic." "I want to show them I am the best person to play this character." These diverse goals can all impede the job of the actor. The goal is to place such inherent imperatives to the side and focus on the work. Naturally, there are times when such goals are healthy and create an ensemble of friendship, professionalism, and mutual respect, but the ultimate goal is to focus on performing the requisite duties of actor unencumbered by personal roadblocks. If you do your job well, then they will: "Like you personally." "Respect your work ethic." "And agree that you are the best person to play this character."

Time away from rehearsals can present moments when you may allow the roadblocks to return based on replaying unsuccessful moments throughout the day in your head. Overblown recounting of the day's proceedings may actually give negative reinforcement to the good work you did do. Actors mentally write their own reviews (usually negative) that overwhelm and stymie the good work achieved. The main question should always be "What do I need to do in order to best portray the requisite needs of the character in order to fulfill his function in the project?" Looking at the function of character in relation to the script and production assuages the heavy burden you may place on your talent and self-worth.

In Exercise 5.2, you will write a review. Each day, and in the third person, review your work with only praise for your process—for example, "— has achieved the beginnings of emotional vulnerability in the climactic scene as she started to understand the high stakes necessary." Despite your humility, focus on the positives as in the last sentence. Then, set goals for the future: "— needs to maintain the freedom she found in the mid-section of the scene throughout." Such an assessment may assist you in achieving a safe rehearsal process with achievable steps to success, rather than continuing to allow negative critiques in your mind.

## Exercise 5.2   Write a positive review

Conflicts between cast members and director may occur within the rehearsal process. This is natural in working on such complex material in such an emotionally vulnerable way. How can the conflicts between your personal self and others not impinge upon your work as actor and character? Categorizing yourself and your co-workers by using the three selves may assist in overcoming your personal roadblocks with another. The issues may be personal on your part. While you may have personal roadblocks with the egotistical lead actor, you must still do your work as actor and character. So you may dislike his self-involved chatter as a person on breaks, but he brings the requisite blowhard quality necessary for Torvald opposite your Nora in *A Doll's House*. Or his disrespectful talk about women as a person may push your buttons, and you will use that to great effect in your climactic speech. Or the problems may be professionally related. He is not doing his job as actor. He has not memorized his lines correctly. He misses entrances. Your professional self knows that it is the director and stage manager's responsibility to speak to him, and therefore, it is out of your hands. Or the issues may be character related; his Torvald is not threatening enough in your interactions throughout the play, therefore you cannot summon the required emotion. By understanding that each actor has a personal journey, which includes his current inability to access the necessary status over you, it may allow you to more honestly explore new territory as Nora. Whatever his reason, and regardless of your needs, your understanding of another actor's issue may allow a better process.

The preview performance process, like the audition process, pushes all involved to heightened emotional territory where the safety of the rehearsal room is now destroyed by the "unfriendly" faces filling up the theater each night or those watching transfixed on the film set, concentrating on your every choice. Your natural reaction is self-preservation. That can also mean an eschewing of the trust, regulations, and expectations mutually agreed upon during the rehearsal process. That shared common goal is superseded by fear and driven by selfish motivation to succeed as an individual rather than as an ensemble. This common roadblock is understandable, but it must also be comprehended in order to achieve necessary mutual trust. All three selves must be focused on the work and not the result. The audience's perceived judgment must be saved for discussions later and not enter into the performance.

The preview period is also a dangerous one for roadblocks as you receive mini-reviews from your friends, family, and peers on the "success" of your work. One off-hand remark can cause an avalanche of self-doubt, as new roadblocks are created or old ones reinforced. Your friend said, "I didn't believe you when you were crying in that one scene." That sentence can cause an actor who has been working steadily to gain the trust necessary for that scene to give up, go back to old tricks, or to spend time obsessively finding ways to creatively "solve" that scene. The roadblock has been restored, and the show can now go on the list of performances that you "struggled with." Despite an innate understanding that this is why you do your work—for the audience—it also can bring your personal acting issues to the surface. For the extrovert, your honest work may be undone by your need to please and desire for acceptance and attention. For the introvert, it may cause you to retreat from your work in order to maintain a safe distance and hide from the audience's attention. Your "need to be liked," your "fear of looking foolish," your "lack of trust" can all be enhanced by adding the audience into your world.

The show opens or the film premieres, and the work is done. If it didn't happen by now, it never will. Opening night means that your performance is as good as it ever will be. Of course, this is not true, but the pressure to achieve perfection in performance on opening night can lead to personal disappointment or false satisfaction. Disappointment may come when a review acknowledges that you never achieved what you aimed for in the performance, despite all your work. Actors must also read each review (if you do so) with the self-awareness most lack when receiving critique on their personal work. Actors must indeed celebrate the praise but also look at its connection to your roadblock. Similarly, actors must also look at negative attention and its relation to your current impediment. So while the opening may bring an end to the rehearsal process, the real work, as artist, can begin in the run.

During the long run of any show, you lose and discover much about the work. The scene that always worked in previews is not landing anymore. You lost a sure laugh. You tried something new and never realized this moment could be played like that. They cried at this moment tonight. All these clues, enhanced by thorough examination throughout a run, are what make an actor savvy. So, while maintaining the performance is certainly necessary, and one of your main responsibilities as an actor, another equally important part of your professional self is to examine how your performance shifts over time. That scene that you always dreaded has become easier. Does this mean that your roadblock can be solved through repetition? Certainly there is a familiarity, and therefore understanding, that enters into a long run. But there is also complacency. Are you short-cutting that scary territory in the run? Have the stakes lessened to make your personal self feel safer in that emotional scene? A constant barometer related to the successes and struggles in your work will allow you to better gauge your performance associated with current or possible future roadblocks.

The closing of a project or the wrap of a film is the perfect time to reassess your journey as an artist. The collection of data related to each project should spur you on to new goals in your work. For example, the shoot of a thirty-second commercial can assist in refining your process and identifying roadblocks. In your toothpaste commercial, the director kept telling you to slow down and smile more. He said your smile looked pained. Ultimately, it was a great experience, and you got a ton of money for it, but you must ponder what you can take away from the notes given and that experience as a whole.

Any project offers a chance "to check in" with regard to your roadblock. What did you learn about yourself? Yourself as actor? And yourself in relation to that character? What were the moments that you are most proud of and why? What were the moments that still rang false to you and why? What were the moments that audiences remarked on most and why? What notes did you keep getting and why? What are your current roadblocks as actor and how can you overcome them? The work of an actor to achieve the open and vulnerable state necessary for unfettered performance is a never-ending process. As soon as one roadblock is overcome, a new one may spring up, usually in unexpected places. That is the journey of an actor—a constant evolving process in relation to your three selves.

## Are There Roadblocks in All Styles?

Roadblocks in various styles, genres, and mediums can appear in ways closely related to the special skills required. No matter the variety, roadblocks for the actor surface in unique ways as the demands to the actor become augmented. The actor's impasse may be redirected, but it remains present. As noted in the "A Note to Actors" introductory section, roadblocks impact the actor's ability to commit fully to any style of acting. This book concentrates on contemporary fourth-wall realism as its basis for acting, since it could be argued it is most ubiquitous, but the concepts and strategies contained within are easily adaptable for any style of acting.

For example, when approaching classical text, where technique is perhaps at the core of your performance, how does a roadblock enter into the approach? Internal roadblocks through timidity related to physical or vocal reticence can hamper good technique. So while all rehearsal and performance notes may concentrate on the externals, there may be internal issues that hamper the actor's ability to showcase their external skills.

Similarly, you may identify as a physical actor whose work comes from action rather than thinking. In this approach, a roadblock may appear when each character you play employs the same pace, energy, and range of motion. Your lack of variety in physical choices hints at a safety zone where a roadblock may be limiting a wider spectrum of possibilities. The question becomes, "Why do I rely on these vetted choices rather than risk to other physical possibilities?" Every actor, even when entering this art form from a different, external perspective, can be hampered by internal issues. Otherwise, these actors would have limitless capacity to portray any role and succeed within each unencumbered. This is simply not the case.

Many musical theater actors experience an expanded sense of selves. There is the personal, the actor, and the character, as well as the singer self and dancer self. The addition of these two selves makes the job even more difficult. Confidence in one area over the other may make the actor self disappear as your singer self shows off your pretty vocal technique. The safety you find in this more highly trained area naturally forces all of the work you have done as actor into a diminished role. A balance between those selves does not occur. For an actor with physical roadblocks, the dancer self becomes embarrassed and self-deprecating during the dance audition because you know you will "never be good enough." Balancing these selves in relation to the special skills required makes this one of the most difficult juggling acts an actor may be asked to carry out. In order to showcase your work to the best of your ability, the musical theater actor seeks a harmonious blending of the five selves.

Acting in a comedy can be seen as a perfect opportunity to work intimately on your roadblock. When appearing in a comedy, you rely on immediate feedback from the audience to gauge the work you are doing. This complicated interaction may be a chance to refine moment after moment, based on the attentiveness of the audience. The actor in the midst of working on a roadblock can feel doubly discouraged related to the immediacy of the situation, if the audience does not respond to what you are working on. The roadblock may force you to lose trust in the work you have been doing in order to push for laughs to gain acceptance. Similarly, if the audience is offering immediate positive reinforcement in terms of laughs, roadblocks may be more easily overcome. Working on a roadblock in a comedy demands deep attention to both audience and self.

More than any other medium, film can be the most paralyzing for an actor with a roadblock. The lack of rehearsal can put you on edge. The proximity of the multitude of cast and crew while you present intimate and vulnerable work can create deep anxiety. The downtime between shots can be a chance for you to lose the connection you had earlier. Shooting out of order can cause you to let frustration rule your acting choices. While all these possibilities could happen, you have the power to not let them affect you. You enter into a film understanding its unique demands, so your choice is to let it affect your work or understand and accept the medium's parameters.

And so it goes with all other styles of acting and genres of work in which an actor addressing roadblocks may find herself. You may choose to surrender to your roadblock or you can accept the special demands. The perfectionist actor is in an absurdist play. The actor with fears of looking foolish is in an old-fashioned melodrama. The actor who lacks trust is in a devised piece. All may choose to surrender to their roadblocks, or they can address them.

# 6    Addressing Roadblocks

*My first roadblock was replacing intimacy with big, generalized emotions. The flip side to this was that I was a very strong and emotional actress. Overcoming this roadblock was especially hard because being a strong performer was something I held onto very tightly. It was (and still is) something I am very proud of, and to an extent, who I believed myself to be as an actress. The first step in overcoming this was understanding that allowing myself to be intimate did not mean that I would never be strong again. It was finding a balance; it was finding a middle. It was understanding that who I am as an actress is not set in stone, nor will it ever be, and that it's okay to change and grow and try new things without fear of losing what I'm already good at. I want to be that actress who brings an audience to tears, the one who acts and reacts from such a deep place within myself it's almost second nature, and in order to do that I have to get out of my own way; this is still something I am working very hard on. Aside from my crippling self-doubt and negative inner monologue, I feel like I did make some progress. I began listening to my scene partners, and I started to see acting as something you put on yourself rather than pull out of yourself, and that really changed my world.*

This chapter shares numerous successful exercises for addressing roadblocks that offer a variety of ways to lessen the power of the barrier to acting. It also includes advice to the educator on how best to create a classroom conducive to this important work.

With a roadblock clearly defined, the actor and teacher now head into territory to weaken its hold on the actor's work. The eradication of the obstruction is an individualized process. For some, simply labeling it immediately extinguishes the barrier, or it disappears without much actual effort. For most though, the roadblock has become an integral part of the actor's process, and it will take time. For those actors, the process can be a long and daunting journey, which will include acting without safety behaviors or dependence on the tricks of the past. Dr. Chris Hopwood notes, "It's a slow transition."

To assist with that slow transition, it is important to set goals across the three selves. For example, my goal as actor and character may be to find vulnerability in my work. So, as actor, I am receptive to the choices that my scene partner is giving me by remaining open and non judgmental. As character, my goal is to be equally open related to the power my partner has over me based on the given circumstances in the script. By setting goals related to your roadblocks, things may start to change. Dr. Jason Moser expands on this: "Things probably aren't going to change immediately. What will change are your goals. So maybe for now, you have this ultimate value of being open or completely vulnerable, completely aware, maybe that's a core value. But you know you can't get to it right now because of x, y, and z, but these are the goals you have." Patience and acceptance in relation to the long process are important qualities to exercise. Moser continues, "You need to be completely aware it's going to take a lot of work on your personal side. Being aware of your core values, but also understanding what goals you can achieve in a certain amount of time, can be really empowering and helpful."

While setting goals can offer empowerment, at certain moments this lengthy process can be met with frustration. This understandable reaction is another way to keep you safe when things may be a bit overwhelming. Hopwood comments, "Maybe the person is too closed off, or maybe the person doesn't want to face their fears. My reaction is, 'So don't do that right away' but ultimately, that is probably where you're going to want to get to—to continue growth." Patience and a clear set of boundaries can alleviate these stressful situations.

Before finding a freedom in your work, this uncharted territory can become stultifying to actors. It might be wise to start with an examination of what the roadblock actually does. If a person avoids vulnerability on stage to keep herself from looking foolish, it actually has the opposite effect. People become acutely aware of the situation. Marika Reisberg explains, "Sadness, the evolutionary emotion of sadness, actually brings people to you. The action is to withdraw from people because you want to be left alone, but actually, it brings people to you." So, the actor who avoids intimacy on stage by making jokes actually draws attention to his limitation. The audience's attention becomes focused on the disparity between text and performance and focuses on the roadblock. The examination of the roadblock as having the opposite effect is one that resonates with many.

Another similar strategy is reminding yourself that your roadblock affects more than just yourself. A roadblock may affect your scene partner by preventing her from achieving her best work, or it may impact the ensemble needed for the success of the production. I worked with an otherwise excellent actor who allowed her roadblock of looking unpleasant on stage to impact the work of a costume designer. The actor lashed out at the costumer, shut down emotionally when she tried on costumes that she felt were unflattering, and offered unwanted suggestions. The director was brought into all future fittings—extra work for others based on an actor's roadblock. Daniel Huston, costume designer, notes:

> I had to alter the execution of my design in an effort to make sure the actor would actually wear the costume the way I wanted. To do this, I had to alter the style of the garments by choosing clothing with different cuts than I originally designed. I also added additional garments that were not in the original design that I didn't completely feel worked for the character. I think that it is very important to make sure that the actor is comfortable in the costumes. However, there is a point where the integrity of the design that has been agreed upon between the director and myself needs to be maintained.

For some, the widespread effect of your personal roadblock may be enough to dismantle it.

Another strategy is to outsmart the roadblock because you understand its manifestation. If it always appears at certain moments or types of situations, you begin to become aware of its pattern. If you are aware that you are about to make the same safe choice or that you won't take a risk in this section of the scene because of your roadblock, you begin to overpower it. Hopwood continues, "A metaphor I've used is football. If you're being blocked to the left, you can probably get around the block to the left, but you won't make the tackle. You have to push into the block in order to have a positive impact."

Sometimes even using the roadblock to propel you to greater emotion can be a clever tactic. If your dissatisfaction with your current choices causes annoyance, you can use that frustration in the scene to allow you to make new discoveries. You may find similar results to the actor discussed in Chapter 5 who used her professional frustrations to propel her character to new levels. You are already being forced into new and surprising work based on your new focus as actor.

Should you be an actor or educator working from a physical perspective, a skills-based approach, or any other non-psychology-based acting methodology, a reinvestment in the externals may reveal personal insecurities hampering a free approach. It can also allow you to take the focus off of the self and place it on your partner or the task at hand. Self-talk that focuses solely on the externals can free some from internal hindrances within physical approaches to acting.

## What Are Some Exercises I Can Do?

Studio exercises are one of the most productive ways to assist actors in safely exploring new territory. Exercises for actors are created to experiment with boundaries of the craft. Moser sees their merit as he describes that, in most people, not specifically actors, there is "a fear of emotion linked to past experiences. Life has convinced us, in brief moments over our lives, through bad habits, sucky periods, and broader beliefs, to create overall narratives where emotion is subverted. And an actor's goal is overcoming their tamped down emotions. These behavioral experiments or exercises create a tolerant accepting of experience where learning opportunities are directly linked to past socialization." Exercises offer a safe and effective way in which to overcome unaccessed emotional availably.

One of the most successful yet difficult exercises to do is a variation of Mel Shapiro's autodrama exercise from his book *An Actor Performs*, which asks an actor to create an extremely personal, autobiographical presentation that theatrically explores a pattern or situation from your life. For a more thorough explanation, you may seek out his book. While the basic outline of the exercise remains the same, for this version of the autodrama, you are asked to theatricalize, in some way, the roadblock that has been limiting your work. The act of theatricalizing the roadblock is freeing to many actors who may choose to sing, dance, or offer unique theatrical methods to perform this exercise. You should avoid personal storytelling and obvious recounting of the origin of the roadblock.

The exercise has been augmented to focus on the roadblock to allow another way of investigating your acting impediment. You will now have to bring it to the fore for presentation. Just as in the original version of the exercise, this roadblocks-based autodrama can explore some highly emotional territory as larger concepts and patterns of one's past are acted out in a theatrical way. And it is not for everyone. Some actors love the chance to examine their inhibitions in acting, while others find it indulgent psychobabble. I have seen the profound successes and recognize its issues.

I had one student (an excellent actor) who did not like to share any part of herself in class or with her theater peers. She wanted her private life kept private, and her time on the stage was where she did her work. For her, the idea of this exercise was torturous. My way of working with her in class was to privately side coach and check in confidentially with relation to the work she was trying to achieve. She eventually vanquished her roadblock in a very private fashion. An autodrama was not the thing for her.

Often this charged material results in overwhelming emotions. Shapiro warns against the difference between a breakdown and a breakthrough. Caution must be used so that the possible epiphanies do not become a benchmark for pushed emotional situations for the class. Actors may be seduced to push to their expressive upper limits. Marika Reisberg cautions that there must be parameters, "Have you been to your upper limits? What measures that? Where is that? Who measures an emotional limit?" In the case of this exercise, the teacher sets the limits.

Jonathon Novello agrees, noting that a culture of high emotion can create dangerous scenarios and mixed signals, "I knew an actor who talked about this idea of a dramatic culture a lot. There was this expectation that you were supposed to be dramatic; you're supposed to be big. All your feelings have to be really big. He feels that because that's the environment, he's supposed to 'perform!'" That culture of high drama may also be related to the environment in the classroom. He continues, "So I wonder how much of this is because you're expected to? You're at school. You're performing for your teacher, you're performing for peers, you're supposed to be here achieving this breakthrough, and it involves this emotional stuff. 'And this is how I get my grade?'" As the consultants warn, this exercise can veer into the personal self and cause actors to push to areas they are unprepared for, so careful guidance focused on the acting issues is necessary. More teaching strategies are contained throughout this chapter.

## Exercise 6.1   Perform an autodrama—an exercise by Mel Shapiro that theatrically explores a theme or pattern in your life related to your roadblock

A student asked me what, as a peer, she was to do with the information shared in the emotionally based work of her fellow students. She understood the motivation for the exercises and benefited from them, but she was unsure about how to interact outside of the classroom with this new knowledge. Reminding yourself that you have gained insight into actor information rather than personal information can assuage that conundrum. It may also be handy to remind yourself that the information shared within the studio should remain safely within the studio. Within the examination of roadblocks actors should be encouraged to exercise not just discretion but also respect for the responsibility related to the process witnessed within one's self and others.

Another equally difficult exercise is from Robert Cohen's *Acting One*, which was designed to access vulnerability. It asks students to pair up, sit on the floor knee to knee, and focus on the other. The initial embarrassed giggles from the partners as someone truly looks at them for the first time are inevitable. But what can happen next is an intimacy and honesty that strips the actors of professional walls or defensiveness and of any tricks or safety behaviors. Consult Cohen's book for a fuller description, but for now, a student describes the exercise and the results for her:

> I remember being so frustrated by my scene until we did a special vulnerability exercise. We were to find a partner, look into their eyes, and truthfully say three phrases: "I can be hurt by you," "I trust you," and "I need you." We were not allowed to say a phrase without complete honesty, and we were to sit silently and relaxed, staring into their eyes. I couldn't believe how hard this exercise was. I sat there bawling at my inability to let someone in. I don't know if I was ever fully able to truly say any of the phrases. The most I was able to get out was a faint whisper, which only happened because I was not the first one to say it. Even with my staggering difficulty with the exercise, it was a turning point for me in becoming an open vessel on stage. Suddenly, I could allow myself to emotionally connect to characters in intense situations. I allowed myself to be an emotional mess, and so I could easily allow my characters to be the same. After that exercise came one of my best moments in scene work.

**Exercise 6.2** "I can be hurt by you" exercise. Using Robert Cohen's exercise, say the following phrases: "I can be hurt by you," "I trust you," and "I need you." You may say those phrases only when you completely believe them

The key to Exercise 6.2 is an honest authentic examination of vulnerability. Students may push to perform or indicate openness, but the goal is an honest openness. Coaching should focus on supportively allowing the student to gain access to truth in the situation. Hopwood hits on the exact challenge for the acting teacher:

> How can I [as acting teacher] tell if a student's being real or not in the way that you're describing—authentic in the actual exercises. Sure, you can tell on some level, "I don't believe what you're saying." How do you do that when levels of behavior just aren't matching up, things they're saying, the look on their face isn't [matching]—there is no cohesion. Think about it from a scientific perspective; you can measure these things, at least in principle, from overall larger contexts.

But alas, in acting you cannot offer such concrete measures. This is the conundrum described in the "A Note to Acting Teachers" introductory section related to the subjectivity of this profession and the personal aesthetic that colors your perspective.

This Cohen exercise was adapted by students who prepared for scene work by sitting in the described fashion and truly looking at their partner. There was no need to repeat the phrases. The version in Exercise 6.3 is an opportunity to lower your defenses from your personal life and begin the work of being a vulnerable actor and layering on the character. It is a chance for an honest, simple check-in to see that you are both available to present your work.

**Exercise 6.3** Honest check-in. Prepare for the scene by allowing yourself to exist in silence with your scene partner

When performing these exercises, or whenever you act, think of your defenses, impenetrability, or roadblock as a coat. This often-used theatrical metaphor is essential to understand the three selves. That coat is necessary in the cold outside world and is there to protect you or to cover your body from harm. When you enter the rehearsal studio, the coat is taken off. The apt metaphor of taking off the coat reminds us that actors must be uncovered when acting. Taking off the coat means their defenses come down or the walls are removed in order to play, connect with another, or allow true vulnerability. When rehearsal is over, the coat is put back on, and the actor leaves the studio to the cold, cruel world.

The coat is necessary because characters live a much more richly emotional existence than most real people in real life. The goal in life is to regularize and manage emotions, while, as character, you have to experience a fuller spectrum of feelings. Dr. Thalia R. Goldstein writes: "Fiction is a simulation of the social world; it's meant to be distilled and simplified. So, characters are therefore necessarily more emotional and less blocked. Every moment of our every day is not exciting or particularly emotional. That's what makes drama and fiction interesting—it's the most extreme moments, the ones that matter, all put into once place." And those extreme emotions require the disrobing of the metaphorical coat. Maintaining impenetrability in personal life is for the personal self, while available vulnerability is for the professional self.

You may avoid the concept of emotional fluidity as a necessary tool for good and honest acting, and rather, approach the work from a practical and external method designed to keep the actor removed from such emotional terrain. And while an actor may not need identification with the character or to experience the inner life of the role in some fashion, the external actor still remains connected to the unregulated mind of the self. The mind can impede a practical approach to acting. Even externally based actors retain an immediate and deeply rooted connection to self when performing; it is nearly impossible not to. In rehearsal, the skills-based actor seeks the same sense of openness and freedom from the negative personal self-talk that the psychologically based actor craves.

Even with the understanding of openness in rehearsal, all the earlier exercises in this chapter can veer to the personal self if not guided correctly. And perhaps there may be no escaping that issue in these exercises. But as with the student above, who was "bawling" at her lack of emotional availability, the work requires careful navigation of emotional territory. Although, as Marika Reisberg asks, "Who can navigate it really well when there is zero modeling for a healthy emotional life?" She suggests allowing enough time, following such highly charged moments within the classroom, for emotional decompression and unpacking. Allow the students to share their reactions to the exercise and take careful stock of their emotional health. Students may take ownership of personal boundaries through the teacher setting the limit and stopping exercises that cross into the personal self or become self-indulgent. They also may be able to better manage the work to be carried out in both the studio and outside. Reisberg continues, "So if you set up the expectation that there is an upper limit it reinforces that there is a boundary we probably need to learn to pay attention to. Because if I go past that boundary, I become ineffective; I become too overwhelmed. And if it looks like I'm hitting that limit, then it's my [the actor's] job, not only as an actor but as a human, that I might need to figure out 'Oh, look at that, that's stuff I need to work on outside of class.'" The boundaries initially set by a teacher will be respected and honored by students. Issues that cross the prescribed boundaries are for a student to address outside of the classroom.

Another effective goal is creating a common vocabulary related to this sort of work. Related to self-regulation, educators can check in with students by offering them a simple one–ten rating system to rate their ongoing work in connection with their roadblock. In uncharted territory, you may sometimes lack the requisite vocabulary to explain your newly accessed feelings. This rating system allows you to simply check in as student or teacher to see how the work is going. Following a scene, a teacher need simply ask, "So, related to the scene, how would you rate your success in overcoming your roadblock?" And a student need only offer a numerical value. You may even want to create a standardized pre- and post-performance evaluation model connected to the level of anxiety the student felt in terms of sharing their work in relation to the roadblock.

Exercise 6.4 is solely focused on your technique as an actor, yet it is a way to strip you of safety behaviors. Experiment with changing your tempo and patterns of thinking while performing the scene at a very slow pace. The educator will offer a constant reminder to slow down the scene and ask you to process the information you receive. This simple act of slowing down the work reminds you to be accessible and open when acting. This seemingly simple adjustment proved terribly difficult for some who had relied on pace to push past vulnerability on stage. The pacing of the scene can be adjusted once the connection is created.

## Exercise 6.4   Slow down the scene

More often than not, when presented with scenes that contain high style, actors will most likely default to playing the scene as realism because it is most similar to everyday life, ubiquitous in stage and film scripts, and the easiest for them to access. When presented with a script that requires style or one that falls into genre-based work (such as camp humor or a horror film), the unique demands of the work can sometimes magnify the roadblock. In this, you must rely on the demands of the style to guide you into new territory in your work, rather than simply an unquantifiable expansion of your realism-heavy arsenal of choices. Like the actor who avoids flamboyant choices for fear of looking ridiculous, they may falter when faced with scripts that require a compliance to the demands of a camp-heavy, outrageous farce. Similarly an actor who is afraid of portraying characters who aren't powerful (such as a terrorized victim in a horror film), must expand his acting based on an understanding the rules each style dictates. Style can expose roadblocks, but more importantly, it can habituate the actor in uncharted territory by simply considering the demands of the style.

**Exercise 6.5**   Style exercise. Act in various styles to expand your understanding of your roadblock and push boundaries

Some actors who avoid deep textual analysis found that another way to address the roadblock was to circle the parts of the script that caused them anxiety. Identifying the moments that created tension or apprehension beforehand is an effective tool for many. Those moments are also a place for the teacher to spend more time coaching. Once identified, the actor can again be the arbiter of success based on their commitment and ability to successfully portray the difficult section of the scene. Even externally based actors can find certain moments vexing, and by identifying them, you can use various technical means to quiet negative internal self-talk.

**Exercise 6.6**   Targeted script analysis. Identify the moments that are most intimately related with your roadblock and circle them in your script

Once you have performed the scene and placed some emotional gravitas on certain moments, you may choose to work solely on these sections through an external approach of pure technique that focuses on physical and vocal production. You may choose to "stair step" your way into the scene, adding incrementally higher emotional output than you have deemed necessary for the scene.

Similarly, offering those viewing the scene a lens through which to view the performance creates an ensemble focused on assisting an actor to identify and target safety behaviors. If the actor feels comfortable enough to share their roadblock and safety behaviors prior to a presentation, a larger group may focus feedback specifically on these areas of success and struggles. Moser notes that, "The technique of focusing on safety behavior or roadblocks with an audience who is in on the evaluation creates a controlled, shared stake in the work."

**Exercise 6.7** Audience lens. Focus viewing and feedback only on safety behaviors and roadblocks

Moser offered a highly clinical variation of Exercise 6.7, with the goal of supporting the actor to understand how the roadblock will or will not be noticed. He suggests, "Bring in a test group. Not theater peers, but people of different backgrounds. Have the actor, without the audience's knowledge, describe what he thinks the audience will see within his performance or what they will be thinking about him during the show. Following the performance, allow the audience to offer feedback." Moser then suggests allowing the actor to poll the audience on various specifics related to the work he was doing. "Did you notice this moment when I lost the connection?" "Did you see me break character and check in with myself at this line?" Targeted and specific questions related to the performance may offer the actor a chance to recognize how obvious or hidden his roadblock and safety behaviors are to an audience.

As you experiment with these exercises, it is essential to keep inspecting your three selves in relation to the outcomes. You may also wish to remind yourself about the personal goals you are setting and the ultimate motivation for the exercises: the elimination of the barrier in performance. Moser notes, "I think that could be a helpful way in keeping a narrative going in some of these exercises. Not just what you want to feel but why you want to feel it and why that feeling makes you feel that way or what it reminds you of. Continuing to ask yourself questions when you do these sorts of exercises can be helpful in continuing the work." So while you are so heavily focused on one aspect of your work, you should certainly continue to assess your progress in relation to the roadblock's destruction, but you should also keep asking yourself why you want to achieve such success. Why is it important for your work as an actor? What is your motivation in relation to your craft?

These first exercises offer short-term strategies of eradicating the roadblock in order to scaffold to eventual freedom in acting. None of the exercises need be too heavily weighted on success or carry such serious implications. In these next sets of exercises, the goal is to find freedom and a sense of play while still targeting the work to be done. Allowing the actor to laugh at the issue also lessens its seriousness for your professional self.

In a run of the scene you are working on, or through a focused improvisation related to the actor's roadblock, allow the actor to exaggerate the symptoms of their roadblock. So, in our earlier example of the student who uses humor to avoid vulnerability, this run will allow him to make every line a joke. The especially intimate moments of the scene should now become highly comedic. The goal is to obviously exaggerate the problem and show the actor the extremes of how his roadblock could manifest itself. Such an exaggeration may lessen the acting issues.

### Exercise 6.8   Exaggerate the roadblock. In a run of the scene or an improvisation, push the roadblock to its extreme

In Exercise 6.9, the actor is asked to perform the scene or improv with a focus on playing the opposite of the roadblock. So, our comedic actor now plays the scene (still in a comedic way) by becoming an overly vulnerable character on stage. His overtly earnest, compassionate, and deeply feeling new version of the character produces, through humor, a glimpse of his requisite future goal of honest vulnerability. The exaggeration or amplification of a comedic/safe version of overt feeling may release the roadblock. By offering these two extremes (such as severe sadness or extreme joy) in Exercises 6.8 and 6.9, the goal is to habituate the actor to better regulate honesty in performance.

### Exercise 6.9   Opposite exercise. Perform the scene playing the opposite of your roadblock

Exercise 6.10 asks you and your scene partner to exchange roadblocks. So, if your scene partner has a roadblock related to rigidity and lacks a sense of play on stage, that is what you will now portray in your performance, while she will take on your comedic covering of vulnerability. The goal is not to mock or exaggerate, but rather, to allow the partner to see their roadblock modeled through another.

### Exercise 6.10   Switch exercise. Take on your partner's roadblock

While many roadblocks are emotional, some roadblocks are external, physical, or vocal manifestations of internal issues. In our example of the actor who uses comedy to substitute for vulnerability, the roadblock may be physicalized in the corners of his mouth as he smiles to block real emotion, or it may be housed in his eyes as he constantly surveys the audience for approval. Vocally, an actor may also feel trapped. Your voice may feel constricted or you may push your voice to avoid interaction. Perhaps you are an actor who shies away from seizing the power in the scene because, growing up, you were told that demanding attention was not a good thing to do. All of these examples are various forms of physical or vocal roadblocks.

Approach this next exercise (Exercise 6.11) in two ways: physically and then vocally. First, do a quick body scan (a full self-examination of the body's energies, aches, and safety behaviors) related to roadblocks. When I concentrate on my roadblock, where do I house tension in my body? Where is the energy emanating from? In the first version of the exercise, examine the physical roadblocks abstractly. Start the movement using a small gesture range, and let it expand and become wilder as you explore the physical limits of this issue. For the actor who felt she was too tall, this exercise could result in jumping up and down to embrace her tall frame and the space within the studio that she may now occupy. In order to exorcise the roadblock from your work, try to physically experiment with abstract movement coupled with uninhibited freedom.

Now, try the same idea with your voice. Physical and vocal "tells" or habits may become readily apparent in this exercise. So, an actor who uses a downward inflection at the end of each line as a safety behavior related to hiding while performing may be forced to vocally uptick, leading to a more dynamic use of the text.

## Exercise 6.11   Physicalize and vocalize your roadblock

Exercise 6.12 requires a willingness to experiment on your part. Using a variation of the "magic if," you will play the scene under the imaginary circumstances: "What if I had no roadblocks?" Acting as if you have no roadblock and embracing the actor you want to be will test your limits and offer a good check-in related to the work you still need to do. This version of the scene is the beginning of "getting out of your own way" covered in Chapter 8. This exercise is for any approach to acting—what if there were no self-imposed impediments that prevent me from fully embracing my craft? Whether internal or external, a removal of the roadblock must be a personal contract.

## Exercise 6.12   "What if?" exercise. Perform the scene as if you had no roadblocks

All the featured roadblock exercises include various approaches to acting beyond psychology-based acting. In Exercise 6.13, a reinvestment in the externals can release any actor from the negative self-talk. Look at the scene dispassionately and identify the technical needs of the scene—what is necessary for the actor to do? What are the physical actions necessary moment by moment? How does this character sound? What special technical requirements are necessary for the scene? In performance, allow only self-talk related to the actions identified as necessary to complete the scene.

## Exercise 6.13    Reinvestment in skills exercise

Approach your work from a new place. If you identify as an actor who works "outside in," who is reliant on external manifestations of the character (walk, clothing, mannerisms), and you find that your work is impeded by self-doubt, then invest fully in working "inside out." Begin transforming your personal self-talk to the thoughts of the character who most likely does not share your insecurities. This opposite way of approaching your work also means that the internally focused actor now remains focused only on externals. So, in this version, you may simply change your walk or body center to see how that may affect the possible self-sabotage-based inner talk. At the very least, this approach frees your work by investing in a new approach.

## Exercise 6.14    "Outside in"/"Inside out" exercise

Choose a "mindless" activity that allows you to detract from your distractions while performing. The activity should be simple in nature and easily repeatable so that it can distract you from negative personal thinking while sending attention to the "doing" of the simple activity. You may choose to find an activity such as washing dishes, brushing your hair, cleaning up your desktop, sorting coins—anything that may be done while still playing the intent of the scene.

## Exercise 6.15    Simple activity focus exercise

Exercise 6.16 reminds the actor to focus solely on the partner. For actors who might fear intimacy, this may simply mean a focus on a detail of the partner's clothing, but for others, it should mean a complete focus on the reaction of the other. All thought should be directed toward how your work is affecting the other. And while this may already be the basis of your approach to acting (as it is for many), roadblocks often do not allow full access to freely observing the other.

## Exercise 6.16   External focus exercise

Another way to relieve you of negative self-talk and allow you to invest in the thought process of the other is to have someone else provide the uninterrupted flow of the character's inner monologue. Have another actor who is aware of the given circumstances of your scene whisper in your ear the imagined inner thoughts of the character. This exercise can retrain you to think within the healthier thought process of the character by removing negative self-talk.

## Exercise 6.17   Inner monologue exercise

Exercise 6.18 offers a chance for actors to write for each other. Implicit in the exercise is that the writer is aware of the roadblock and its manifestation in the actor's work. If this is not the case, allow the writer to interview the actor in relation to her roadblock statement and moments in performance where it has appeared. Then, allow the writer to write a monologue or scene that directly addresses the roadblock in a theatrical fashion that will force the actor to examine current limitations. The monologue should not be a biographical or literal explanation of the barrier within the actor, but rather, a fictional character and theatrical monologue or scene that explores the identified emotional territory that boldly forces the actor into a new way of working. If it is a monologue, allow the actor performing to cast another actor from the studio as the person they are addressing in the piece. The other actor should be cast based on their ability to make the actor feel comfortable enough to overcome the roadblock, or to offer a relationship that reflects the emotional needs necessary in the newly written piece. When performed, the monologue or scene should be memorized and rehearsed and prepared for coaching. This allows time for the actor to spend time personally working on the roadblock prior to sharing it with others.

## Exercise 6.18   Write a monologue for your partner

Exercise 6.19, the "universal scene," can be quite difficult but it is highly effective when used with a group of actors working on their roadblocks. Give all actors the same two-person scene and have them learn it separately. When this is done, ask them to perform the scene as a group with two actors beginning the scene as normal. Whenever a line is dropped or a connection is lost, one of the two actors performing the scene will be "tagged out" by one of the actors who is observing. The actor who forgets the line or drops the connection may be replaced or may self-select out of the performance. A new actor enters the scene, and the remaining partner must now respond to the new partner's choices. This process takes several attempts to truly master, but the idea of responding to different choices forces an actor to bravely access new choices spurred by the various partners. The universal scene is a great way to shake from within them actors' stuck patterns. Because it lacks rehearsal, the universal scene demands a lessening of the stranglehold actors have on their own work and encourages freedom and play. It also maintains a specific structure sometimes lacking in improvisation. In Exercise 6.19, actors are forced to be daring while they address their roadblock.

## Exercise 6.19    Universal scene

Moser notes, "One way to identify roadblocks is through expressive focused and targeted journaling." Rather than simply notating your feelings and experiences, target the journaling related to your roadblock and its daily appearances. He also offers a similar strategy to access emotion. In the following example, Moser was responding to a student who avoided sadness in most characters that she played:

> The first thing you can do is walk around your daily life and notice some twinge of sadness and notice those patterns when you feel that type of sadness. Then, you can start to build ideas like, these are the things that really do trigger sadness for me; I can draw on that. A Kleenex commercial that always brings me sadness, "Why the hell is a Kleenex commercial making me so sad?" "I get teary when I see stories of people overcoming adversity, I can't help it, I get teary." So then you have these times, these moments you can come back to as one way of knowing sadness. On a daily, weekly basis, sit down and invite sadness in, using these scripts [the collected moments of sadness] where you are literally sitting and meditating on sadness. You can use that script to continue to ask why, what, and where did it come from. So you can have meditation or self-monitoring experiences where you are paying much more attention than you used to throughout the day.

These strategies can translate to a myriad of roadblocks, whether it is intimacy, vulnerability, self-esteem, or any of the other issues contained in this book.

**Exercise 6.20** Targeted journaling. Write or "invite" reflection related to your roadblock

Another form of helpful exercise is pre- and post-performance journaling. In this sort of writing, you may share your worst fear about the upcoming performance and then your reaction to your work subsequently. You can set goals for each performance as a sort of contract. Moser suggests journaling in response to the question, "What is the worst that can happen in your upcoming performance?" He offers a few examples: "People throwing tomatoes at you; you slip and fall off stage; people are laughing, tweeting all over the stratosphere. You're the laughing stock of the entire world—play that out. It's the worst possible ending." Examine those possibilities (extreme and practical) before the scene begins, and then do feedback afterward. Did your predictions come true? More than likely, your worst fears were not realized. This simple trick is another way to diminish the roadblock.

**Exercise 6.21** Pre- and post-performance journaling about your worst fears. Examine what is the worst thing that could happen if you do not perform the scene as you intended

One final variation of journaling asks you to write as character. While this is a common actor technique, the focused and targeted journaling should surround the character's experiences with the actor's roadblock. The writing should examine, in detail, how the character addresses the limitations that currently plague the actor.

**Exercise 6.22** Journal as character

In this final exercise (Exercise 6.23), close your eyes and meditate on your imagined fuller self as actor—an actor who does not fear the work contained in the roadblock statement. Ask yourself, "What is the worst thing that can happen if I commit fully to this work?" Is the answer that you will look foolish or fail? What if that occurs? Is the answer that you will lose the temporary respect of your peers? What if that occurs? Then they may not like working with me. Continue to ask "What if?". Keep examining the worst-case scenarios until you have diminished the roadblock's power. Now, meditate on the best-case scenarios using the same "What if?" technique. What if I overcame my roadblock?

## Exercise 6.23    Meditation. Spend sometime thinking about the actor you want to be

In all the exercises, the focus is on an examination of the roadblock related to the craft. It is hoped that all actors have, in some minor form, experienced circumventing their impediment successfully. But the work asks for you to harness and amplify those successes based on the given circumstance in the script. And for some, this causes confusion.

## Why Can't I Overcome My Roadblock?

More than likely, your initial work will contain a blend of missed connections with a scene partner or sloppy attempts to connect emotionally to the work you want the most. You may find uncertainty in your physical and vocal technique that still remains guarded by critical self-doubt. This is because you are hyper-sensitive to your roadblock's power over your craft. As you begin to work in this new area, you will notice a lessening of the observational monologue in your head and begin to concentrate on the things you wish to focus on, such as your scene partner and the given circumstances. The subtle dance that the actor's mind does, normally gliding between personal, professional, and character, will be askew in these early stages and that is perfectly valid. You will return to a more mindful state of acting as the bridge to the work you wish to do gains stability.

Throughout the process, an actor may feel overwhelmed by the deep reflection. Novello notes, "In very few professions do the critiques of director or teacher and immediate feedback from audience shape your view of honesty in performance." This difficult and anxiety-ridden state of continuous examination causes an actor to work in a constant state of self-reflection and at times this may be overwhelming especially when dealing with a roadblock.

Moser notes other possible impediments to fully committing to work including, "losing themselves forever in a role, avoiding emotion, fearing negative evaluation, saving up the full emotion for the next run, or waiting for your scene partner to make the first move." All of these and other reasons circumvent the work you wish to be doing. When distilled, the main reasons for you not being able to currently overcome your roadblock fall into three basic categories: safety, anxiety, and overthinking.

## Safety

An actor's wish to remain safe is a natural reaction to new experiences. You, as a person, do not naturally seek out areas of discomfort, so the reticence with which an actor approaches work on roadblocks makes perfect sense. Safety includes your performance zone in which you have made all former acting choices. It is comfortable. It is comforting. It is where you "live" on stage. Expanding that zone to include new choices, honest interaction with a scene partner where none had been, and a lack of rigidity in performance automatically make you feel unsafe. You want to protect yourself—a natural reaction.

Marika Reisberg questions, "What are you protecting? Does it mean you must free the voice or movement? Making a connection to yourself, to your scene partner, or to the environment you are in? Cognitive thought-changing stuff?" And your answer may be a singular focus or may be that you are protecting all those things. The first step is to get to the heart of the matter of where and why you do not feel safe in certain aspects of performance.

A lack of safety causes actors to seize up and pinch their work rather than offering the freedom of release that comes with a more holistic level of safety. Jonathon Novello has seen this before: "I've worked with actors over the years, a number of actors. They seem to struggle about the faith, about putting it all out there. Is it blind faith? Or it seems that sometimes it's part of the culture—like there's an expectation that I'm supposed to put all of myself out there. And if I don't, I can't act. And I'm not able to get that far along [in my acting] because I am starting from a fear-based place." The fear-based place that Novello speaks of is quite the opposite of safety. Safety and fear, these polar opposites, are intertwined in an actor examining roadblocks. For those who allow fear or tentativeness to guide them, remember that, for an actor, the emotional state is transient. A similar recognition of the transient quality of the vocal and physical demands of the skill-based actor may also nullify negative self-doubt.

Safety also includes a sense of trust created by the shared examination of the roadblock. Trust that the teacher and fellow actors who have gained insight and information related to your struggles with roadblocks will keep that information within the classroom or rehearsal hall. By intimately understanding yourself in relation to the craft, and performing complex work such as the autodrama exercise (6.1), you may share private elements that impact your work.

## Anxiety

Moser stated in an interview, "Actors are highly anxious as their internal focus constantly causes anxiety." The inward focus can, in many ways, initially inhibit your craft, as you constantly assess your work based on your roadblock statement. Your anxiety has various forms and motivations and must be examined to discover your personal relationship to it. The already understandably anxious actor may have a newfound level of worry by recognizing your professional work has areas of limitations. You may compound the anxiety by not immediately finding success in overcoming your roadblock. As private and personal issues surround it, your worry may be heightened as you get closer to the emotional core of what causes your roadblock. Begin to examine your own personal anxiety's manifestation in your professional self.

As human beings we are not usually conditioned to expose vulnerabilities in front of a group of strangers. It may be at odds with everything that we have been taught or experienced. Evolution has not prepared us for such things. Special cultivation of skills is necessary for this unique profession that asks an actor to be calm and open in highly anxiety-producing situations. For some, recognizing and embracing this unavoidable anxiety is enough to allow the actor more freedom in performance.

The consultants offered various strategies to overcome the increased anxiety that may be impeding you from achieving success. So, as you prepare to present a scene, your thoughts may go to the great work of your fellow actors and, in comparison, the lousy job you might do; you begin to experience the sweaty palms and shoulder tension that results in shortness of breath, or causes an unstoppable shaking in your leg. Begin to examine not only its effects, but its cause. Once identified, your goal is to discover the individual tactic for you to overcome the enhanced pressure you are creating for yourself. Perhaps even realizing that you are responsible for this unnecessary pressure may lessen your anxiety; but if not, other strategies are offered.

When you feel the anxiety begin, make sure you try to do a body and emotional scan. This concept of examining the body for any signs of tension is an excellent way to see where and how the pressure insinuates itself physically, and in turn, into your psyche. At the first sign of unease, your stomach may tighten. This is the moment to examine the actual physical symptoms and how, specifically, they present themselves within your body, how else your body may store tension, and any safety behaviors you may be employing. Similarly, it is also the time for a mental scan of the event that triggered the worry, the self-talk that is happening in your brain related to the event, and the patterns that may be occurring in your work as a result of anxiety. Understanding your anxiety from these vantage points may assist you in vanquishing unwanted worries in performance.

Most actors may wish to quickly suppress the anxiety when they feel it beginning, but the consultants warn that the act of suppression or strangling the anxiety may actually create additional stress. Rather than suppression, examine the concept of simply trying to turn down the volume in your head. As stated earlier, actors are anxious, and some level of unhealthy, anxious self-talk may remain at all times, so redistribute mental focus away from smothering anxiety and simply try to turn the volume down.

Two concepts mentioned earlier in combination may assist. The third-person self-talk blended with an awareness of an acceptance (like the ACT technique discussed in Chapter 4) of the stress-filled situation may be a way to regulate anxiety. So rather than "I am going to mess this up!" it becomes "Rob is going to do the best he can with what he prepared." Perhaps even retraining that self-talk to positive thinking may assist. So instead of "They are doing so great and I will mess this up," it becomes "Rob can do this! Rob is ready!" It becomes a way to, as Moser notes, "Reappraise and reinterpret. That boosts your ability to get back out into the external world again and start paying attention to things out there instead of the stuff in your head." Retraining or reinterpreting the way in which you think about anxiety-ridden situations is the key to removing the paralysis related to your roadblock. This seems the ultimate goal for any actor ruled by anxiety.

Moser also has pointers about anxiety related to the classic response that most offer of "just breathe." Rather than concentrating on the inhalation, he says, "It's actually the exhalation process that's more important. You take a normal breath in, and the real important part is letting a long breath out because now what you are telling your body is, 'I don't need that much oxygen, I'm cool. I can breathe all this air out because it's very calm, and I'm safe and there is no problem.'" By focusing on the specifics of this type of breathing, the actor can also distract the anxiety.

The consultants also suggest creating a strategy that generates a hierarchy or delineation of anxiety related of the three selves. Create an understanding of anxiety within your personal self, your professional self in performance or rehearsal, and your character's relationship with anxiety. By delineating these marked differences between selves, you may be able to best manage the anxiety through nuanced understanding. For clarity, you may want to journal about or meditate on these differences. Understanding the variations of anxiety between the three selves, and clearer time spent defining and exploring each of them, can lessen anxiety.

The above examples can assist with generalized performance anxiety; those moments of stage fright understood even by nonactors who have never set foot on a stage. But anxiety related to your roadblock is sometimes more specific. It may be anxiety related to accessing vulnerability on stage, apprehension of a particularly intimate scene, or trepidation related to trying out choices that make you uncomfortable. These solely actor-based fears require actor-based solutions. Should your anxiety persist, consult the more targeted strategies in the next chapter.

Hopwood notes that anxiety-inducing matters for actors may "be more intrapersonal [between self and mind] than interpersonal [between self and others]." He suggests "looking to see if the basis for the anxiety is cultural [the energy in the room] or dispositional [your personal mood]." He also suggests that a detailed examination of your contribution to the anxiety may lessen its power. Further, the interplay between the three selves requires a larger teasing out of the information.

While I have written much about the intrapersonal and the dispositional, the interpersonal and cultural may have just as much affect for some when it comes to roadblocks. This could mean that you may have some intimidation related to the director or teacher in the classroom. It could mean that you place more value on your classmates' responses than your own. It could be an unsettling peer-to-peer relationship that causes trepidation in the classroom. These issues may likely be resolved through honest conversation about the issues you feel. By offering solutions on how to adjust the relationships to more advantageous interactions, you may be able to showcase the work you know you are capable of. However, this repeated pattern in various studios, productions, and interactions hints at intrapersonal roadblocks.

## Overthinking

One of the main pitfalls of having to spend so much time analyzing your connection to your craft is overthinking. As an actor the mere goal of seeking peak performance is a contract with self-examination. Therefore, it is extremely common for actors to "get stuck in your head" when doing this highly reflective work.

The consultants noted that this common problem is an attachment to the outcome and not the process. An actor who overthinks is so committed to the ultimate goal (to overcoming your roadblock) that you ignore the careful steps necessary for achieving it. Your focus on your ultimate performance removes any possibility from accomplishing it, since you are focused on the future rather than the present. You have removed yourself from the basic tenets of listening and responding.

Another concept put forward by the consultants as a reason for overthinking is intellectualization. Intellectualization is an avoidance of experiencing emotion through a reliance on discussion and rationalization. This concept is actually a safety behavior, as it removes you from having to access the feeling and allows you to keep yourself safe by simply talking about the issue through emotionless rationalization. A way to combat that, as educator or actor, is to stop the discussion and begin to scaffold up incrementally to higher emotional commitment and intensity. Rather than allowing the actor to distract through intellectual analysis, simplify the coaching and limit the pre- and post-performance discussion in order to focus on the understanding of the emotion. Spend time on slowly adding more emotional heft and risk to your choices and rely less on rationalization.

Moser notes that overthinking is only natural in that it is how the brain functions and how we are wired. So rather than deal with emotion as an actor, he notes, "Part of it is because that's what your brain is built to do. Your brain is built to make stories, make sense out of things you don't understand, but if you overindulge that mechanism ... it can have backfiring effects where you get lost and you get stuck." The actor remains "stuck in your head." Removing that phrase from the actor working on roadblocks is a difficult process. Even a physical approach to acting may become unhinged as the actor concentrates on personal-based issues that hinder true physical freedom.

The idea of overthinking seems a common and understandable response to uncharted territory. If that information does not relieve the pressure and quiet the brain when performing, there are several strategies to employ. Use music as a distraction prior to your performance; a pair of headphones and the right playlist can divert your attention until the director calls, "Action!" Similarly, a quick scan of imagery you have collected related to your character can refocus you and allow you to reinvest in healthier thinking. A quick examination of the given circumstances can also direct you to the desired thoughts prior to entrance. Concentrate on the objective. Concentrate on details on the film set or backstage—whatever can distract you from the negative inner monologue playing out in your head.

For some, nothing other than "solving" this riddle will quieten their brain. The need for answers to newly accessed emotion in the professional and the personal quest for understanding may lead some actors to delve even further into the origin of their roadblock. This work can most certainly cross into the personal, but for some, the unanswered question, "Where did this roadblock come from?" must be answered.

The consultants pointed me toward one commonly used Cognitive Behavioral Therapy tool that might offer assistance: the "downward arrow technique." This is similar in structure to the "What if?" exercise (6.12). This technique is used to get at the core beliefs or issues of a patient, but can be adapted easily for the roadblock and the actor. In this rather straightforward technique, you should examine the issue—frustration with not being able to get past your roadblock in acting class. In your version of the downward arrow technique, you identify the roadblock and then identify the first reason you believe you cannot overcome your barrier. Once that is identified, you keep examining until you get to the core issue or origin of the roadblock.

Using the example of the actor who substitutes humor to avoid intimacy on stage, he begins with his roadblock statement. He must then ask,

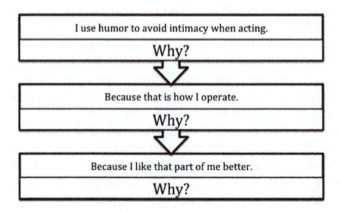

**Figure 6.1   Downward arrow technique**

"Why?" His answer may be "Because that is how I operate? " Then, again, "Why?" His answer may be "Because I like that part of me better?" Then, "Why?" (see Figure 6.1). The process continues until you get to the heart of matter, which may be a fear that the audience may reject him if he exposes his true self. It may be that your elementary school teacher who told you that you couldn't act traumatized you, and you have been trying to prove her wrong ever since. Or it could stem from a lack of confidence that infects all interactions, both personal and professional. All roadblocks are usually based on some trauma, event, or upbringing that created the blockage. Trauma can range from small recent experiences to weighty unremembered events or feelings; it may be habituated behavior or defense mechanisms. The trauma may also be deeply rooted in all three selves—for example, an experience related to your personal self that caused your motivation to begin acting and has affected the types of role you play. In some cases, the discovery may be too much for you to currently handle.

In moments like these, work beyond the acting studio may be necessary. As always, the goal of the actor is to mine rich, emotional territory while keeping a safe and healthy distance in your work. As mentioned, the professional and character roadblock may bleed into the personal. This is not the purview of this book or your acting teacher. However, you may need to seek assistance to help clarify such interlacing and overlapping issues. More than likely, a therapist can help you with the multitiered examination of your three selves. Again, this temporary feeling is the next step to building the flexible and open artist you want to become.

## What Is the Best Way to Teach about Roadblocks?

For this section, I decided to include a lengthy conversation related to the unique aspects of teaching acting. I posed provocative questions to the consultants on the book to gauge their opinion on everything from ethical boundaries to classroom management. I found their responses fascinating and wanted to share them. Also in attendance was graduate student, Matthew Greenbaum.

**Roznowski:** In teaching such a uniquely personal craft, what is the best way for the teacher to reach the student?

**Hopwood:** The way that I teach, I feel like part of the aspect of the relationship has to be personal. My students have to be able to look me in the eyes and know that I care about them, so that way, if I say "you're messing up right now," they don't hear "I think you're bad person; I don't think you're good enough; I'm going to reject you." They hear, "Someone that I trust and care about and whose opinion I respect is telling me something that I should learn from." My own feeling is that you have to have somewhat of a personal relationship so that you can have trust, so you can navigate that. And then the teacher might say, "Now it's time for you to go on your own, and I can't help you, so go ahead. I'm not going to be there for you, but we can talk about it later." And sometimes you have to say "Come to my office. I've got to tell you what you're doing that's not working," so that there's trust there. I tend to have relatively more personal—again it's not so personal that I cross a boundary—but some personal relationship. Because, otherwise, I would not know how to do my job. I think another way to do it is to be dominant, and kind of not care, and say, "Take it or leave it; either you're going to learn from me or not," and leave the responsibility to the other person. That could work too because that can be what they expect, and then they know that this is how this person is and they are good at their job. A person with that kind of approach might say it doesn't matter if you and your student care about one another or not.

**Roznowski:** And the hard part about that, I would imagine, as a therapist or teacher, is that you in fact know what the roadblock is but you can't say that to someone, can you?

**Hopwood:** Well, I think it is more a question of "Do you know?" But I think that most people, if they take the time to stop and reflect on what is happening and why, can figure it out for themselves. I have a hard time imagining that whatever roadblocks they are having as actors don't have a very direct parallel in their personal lives. And yet it is not my job or Rob's job to help them manage their personal lives. So I think that for Rob to notice that the trigger is happening, it is not your job to say, "This is what I think it means. This is what I think you can do about it." But I do think there is a role for people like us to say, "I think that that is happening again," and the actor's job is to say, "Okay, let me figure out what that is." I want to notice it, observe it, and help them observe it, so that they can understand it and then, if they understand it, usually they will stop doing it.

**Novello:** You're an acting teacher. You don't need to solve it.

**Moser:** Right. Give them a little bit more empathy. And then say, "So, here are some numbers for people who can help."

**Roznowski:** How would you manage a classroom addressing roadblocks?

**Reisberg:** I taught a class in a graduate psych program that was not therapy, but every student thought it was. So I had to address that and redirect their focus. I had this little handout called "Being a Good Group Member" that gave them some instructions and rules about: Is what I'm sharing important for the group? Is what I'm sharing furthering the group? When you work with a group of actors, you are a team. You're a collection of people. So that strategy can assist.

**Novello:** And there's a level of how you're supposed to commit to the project.

**Reisberg:** I talk a lot about knowing upper limits. How much can I share and still be present and function and manage what I'm sharing? But is what I'm sharing too much for the group? And so I have to track that as well because I'm a part of the group.

**Moser:** I think part of this is going to be up to the individual teacher, in terms of style and having some sort of note on the syllabus that lays out these ground rules. I don't know how you're going to phrase any of these things, but talking about time management and if things get too personal you will have to move on.

**Hopwood:** Part of the issue also is when you set ground rules, how much do you then spend your time monitoring?

**Novello:** Right, so, "I have to remember these ground rules. What if I do this? What if I do that?" Then you cut someone off and then there's shame because you can't violate the ground rules. So, I think this is something that depends on how much you want to take on in terms of making the decision in the moment.

**Moser:** As opposed to having things explicit in the beginning. There are going to be costs to any strategy. There's a cost to preempting things by potentially missing something from some person. But the cost of not having some of those things on the syllabus might be greater because then you're having then to wiggle too much on the fly, and things are going awry, and you don't have a handle on the group or an individual student.

**Roznowski:** Sometimes I think, "That person's so close to breaking through to what their issue is." And then I ask, "Does anyone in the group mind if I spend more time with the person?" That's already a loaded question.

**Greenbaum:** To some extent, you have to be attached to the outcome if you know that there's that limit. What if the emotional state of the character lives beyond that limit?

**Roznowski:** Like you have to give birth on stage. You have to murder someone.

**Reisberg:** I think expectations in terms of defining this upper limit; at times it is okay to violate it. And we expect that you'll violate it. And so, a lot of it, for me, is that there's going to be a level of acceptance for mistakes violating some aspects of the code because you can't control these things. In some of these ways, you're trying with the mindfulness being in the present moment, focused, with nonjudgmental awareness; you're going to lose control in some of those instances. I also think that the sort of safe space setting is that you're not going to be punished for violating any of these things. These are the expectations; this is the code of conduct. There are upper limits, but you might violate them, and that's going to be okay too, but there's contingency in that—you know what's going to happen if you exceed that limit. So I think a lot of it, too, is that we're going to accept that it might get hairy sometimes.

**Moser:** Even if you reach that upper limit, maybe the definition of that upper limit that was set up was actually the wrong one. And, sure, by the books, it seemed like you overdid it, but you actually got to where I wanted you to go, now maybe I need to adjust, you know, my upper limit next time because I see where it can benefit some people, or maybe it's okay, that it benefited them. So flexibility and acceptance are important. I think everyone can agree that it seems fair that, in the moment, there has to be flexibility even if you make it explicit to the group, but if you don't make it explicit, then at least you know that's the rule in your head—the process of learning how to pay attention to boundaries and setting up those dynamics, too. It says, "I have to monitor myself. I have to think about this as teacher."

**Novello:** Because it changes the dynamic of things. And then if one person's taking too much attention, and it looks like somebody needs to say something, work something, I'll say, "You know what, you've got a lot to talk about there, and it's really important. And I don't want to take time away from this group because I'm afraid it's going to pull me into something else, but how about you and I chat for a minute afterwards?" and finish that conversation. So it acknowledges the moment without really pathologizing it. But it also doesn't take time away from the group, and then it gives that person sort of that validation—"Okay. What I'm saying is important and there's a place to put it." I think the danger of "Whoah, that's too much" is probably where it is tricky for you because there's not a clear spot to put it.

**Moser:** In therapy groups, I have skills training groups in the VA [Veterans Affairs] with Vietnam Vets, and I still have this issue. I only have so much time in a session. I have eight guys at the table, and I can't spend thirty minutes on one guy. I just can't.

**Hopwood:** So it might not be about boundaries; you might have people who won't shut up about it but then, as a teacher, you might notice that too. And you can pull them aside and say—.

**Moser:** It comes back to who's responsible.

**Roznowski:** But can't that be student and teacher?

**Reisberg:** It is, and I think a lot of times students have an expectation that it is all on their teacher to hold the safety because they set up that it is "a safe space." Like, as a student, I can't move throughout my whole life and expect external safety to manage me. Then we get back to what's safety. And I think everybody has their own structure of what safety is.

**Roznowski:** Someone might say, "I felt unsafe when you asked us to share." And then other people say, "Wow, that made me feel really safe."

**Moser:** [Things have come up in my class] where somebody might be sharing too much, but, I put what I call "a disclaimer," essentially I can lay out who I am and my lens, so this is what you're going get. I lay it all out. I'll say, "so if you're wondering how I'm going to present some information, now you have a sense." I think a lot of it is responsibility and as long as you're clear and transparent about what your class is going to be like and how you approach things, then you're doing your due diligence.

**Roznowski:** But would that lens for an acting teacher be, "Here's what is honest acting to me: to me this is vulnerable acting?" Is that too much to ask as an acting teacher, to say, "Here's what I respond to because basically my job is to monitor emotion?"

**Novello:** Teaching acting is really neat, right. This isn't math. I mean [students] go to math class and can be completely internal all of the time. You're not out there. You're not exposed—in public in front of every peer. You can be miserably failing in that class and conceivably, no one knows. And that's the majority of the experience. But in acting [the student] is out there. And it's expected. So it's an interesting thing to teach them because you're dabbling in an area that has a great potential to wander down into these scary places.

**Reisberg:** Right? Without the equipment to deal with that.

**Roznowski:** When you get to that place, and you're confronted with something that someone wants to overcome, what do you do when you're not equipped?

**Reisberg:** You create a container. And there are expectations that are held in the container. And as a teacher, you are responsible for holding them in. If a student crosses that boundary, it's up to you to say, "I'm going to have to have to put the brakes on here. We crossed this line. I'm going to name it, and if we need to address it further, we'll do that outside of class. We're going to come back to this specific thing we've been working on." My experience in acting school was that students would get to a certain place and the teacher would say, "They're so close. Let's keep going! I can't stop them, they're in the moment." And so when weighing the benefit and cost of that in the moment, how do you navigate it? I think basic therapeutic skill training for acting teachers is the answer.

**Moser:** To learn how to maintain and set boundaries with language.

**Reisberg:** Offer some really concrete things because I know, in a lot of movement classes, especially in the beginning of movement classes, when people who haven't experienced a lot of movement are paying attention to their bodies, a lot of stuff comes up and emotional breakdowns happen, and how do we come back to the present moment? How do we know that this isn't the time or space to explore that? I like the technique you mention in the book of naming the things in the room. [See Chapter 7.] That is really helpful.

**Roznowski:** What if the teacher tries to "fix" them?

**Moser:** You're not the expert.

**Novello:** I'm not the expert in their life. They're the expert in their life. I just get to witness it and reflect some things back and comment.

**Reisberg:** And give some proper space for this stuff.

**Hopwood:** Right, the question is, are the things you are doing that get you to your goals consistent with your own values?

**Roznowski:** But then you have this outside eye [the teacher] saying, "That's not true, that's not honest." And the actor responds, "But it's worked in my personal life, and now in my professional life you're telling me it's not honest."

**Novello:** Or is it just not working for that professor?

**Moser:** And that's why I think it's important to say. The idea about a disclaimer is that they need to also know this is all subjective, right? It's just one person's vote over another. There is a way for you to communicate that with them—that there are masses that either agree or disagree with your portrayal. We can't all agree on who good actors are; we can agree on some, but then we can disagree on others.

The transcript addressed several subjects related to classroom management, ethics, boundaries, and a teacher's subjective understanding of the student's work in relation to the roadblock. These important topics, and your responses to them, can define your methodology. For the most part, our psychological approach to teaching acting can be better informed by these mental health experts.

"Trust" and "freedom" are two words most often used by acting teachers when creating their classroom environments. Trust is mutual, and educators must trust that their students are willing to explore their roadblocks. Freedom comes from a willingness to play and experiment with tested and untested materials. Unless clearly defined by the educator, these two words remain subjective terms.

Subjectivity must be examined through a personal lens. Educators must also explore their personal roadblocks and how they affect their professional selves. While you may have a personal roadblock of abhorring laziness due to past personal experiences, you must also make certain that this does not impact your work in the classroom. Using that example, you must explore your impatience with students who do not carry out the work the way you would, your supplying of the answers rather than allowing students to give them to you because you are almost certain they have not completed the reading, your low expectations for their success, or your constant complaints about them to your peers. Just as actors must explore the crossover of professional and personal interactivity of roadblocks, so must educators. Only then can a classroom of freedom and trust occur.

A classroom's management also affects the ability to address road-blocks in an actor's work. Actors who need rules and rubrics in order to feel safe are in complete contrast to those who fear the final, graded presentation. The classroom without consequences can also horrify those dependent on the safety of rules, while strict guidelines can stifle others who need the freedom to create. Having the skill to traverse both sides of the spectrum related to the individual is vital for a productive learning environment.

Just as there are introverts and extroverts, no one actor learns in the same way. So while, for some, improvisation may be the entrance into overcoming roadblocks, to others, journaling may prove the ultimate approach. The introvert/extrovert classroom model is something that is genuinely thought-provoking in theater—a profession filled with many introverts. An examination of theater's reliance on improvisation, par-ticipation grades, and ensemble building may need reformation related to the revolution Susan Cain calls for in her work on introversion. Too often the model of the first volunteer, the loudest in the exercise, or the leader of the group is rewarded while introverts are just as invested though not nearly as gregarious.

Actors are innately people pleasers. They love applause and laugh-ter. More often than not, they will also try to please their educators or look to their peers for approval. This need must be constantly exam-ined during the coaching process for roadblocks. Knowing when to address their impasses and when to delay is terribly important. Actors are keenly sensitive, so teachers of acting must be as well. Guiding a stu-dent who is exploring difficult material into highly emotional territory must be done with caution. Knowing when to end the exercise, when to not push the student for feedback, or when to break the tension of the moment requires great empathy. Similarly, knowing when to push a student in whom you see potential must also be explored. As always, addressing roadblocks requires buy-in from the student and educator who must constantly check in through verbal and nonverbal cues as to where to go next in the work.

# 7    Roadblocks Expanded

*It was confirmed through several of the tests that I am someone who has high levels of anxiety, something I have known for a long time. What I didn't know was that my anxiety is also a large contributing factor to the way I see myself, and that it is actually possible to overcome this. At the beginning of the semester, I felt insecure in rehearsal spaces and unable to bring the same energy I brought to auditions/callbacks; a space I felt controlled. Once in rehearsal, feeling the pressure of continually making new choices and offering the vulnerability that a rehearsal environment requires, I would close off and withdraw. I felt I was only able to present the bare minimum of work necessary to keep up with the process but not put myself out there too far. I also found I have issues with control and will often "direct" my scene partners. This issue does not come from a desire to control the scene, but a need to feel safe by controlling what someone else is going to be doing to me. In some scene work, I felt unsafe with my scene partner due to the intensity of the material, so I held back physically in the scene to avoid meeting my scene partner halfway, therefore pulling back his performance as well. Addressing this has completely changed the way I see myself as an actor and as a person. I am now working diligently to focus on thinking of my own performance and taking what my scene partner gives me openly. By fully committing to staying invested in the given circumstances of the time period, the moment before, and the personality of my character, I have enough work on my hands to create an honest character rather than control what my scene partner is doing. I am now able to brand and present myself better in the rehearsal room without the fear that everyone will automatically judge or dislike me. My thoughts of myself as an actor now mean more to me than anyone else's in the room, which has already taken me places I never thought I'd reach.*

In the above testimonial, you can note that the actor used several of the categorizations for roadblocks which are covered in this chapter, specifically: anxiety, vulnerability, judgment, and body awareness. You may note that your roadblocks stem from such a cross-section. Using the exercises from the last chapter, as well as the strategies suggested within this one, you may find your personal solution for finding freedom within your work.

Much has been written in other books about self-imposed barriers related to various types of performance, but what makes this section unique is its focus on how these matters manifest themselves in actors. This chapter can be used for actors or educators to spark discussion and inspire both to research further. In each section, there will be an overview of the issue related to its manifestation in acting, questions to consider as actor and educator, strategies for overcoming the roadblock, and finally, supplementary reading to study. Throughout this chapter, consultants offer insight, advice, and tactics to confront the roadblock. Since most issues covered in this book are emotionally based roadblocks, you will note a greater reliance on the consultants' expertise presented as direct quotes throughout the chapter. Note that not all suggestions and theories will work or should be tried by all. As always, when approaching your professional work, choose the examples that resonate best with you or fit your current roadblock.

This section deals with the immediate roadblock and not its root or cause. More often than not, the cause must be traced back to your personal self, which is not the purview of this book. The cause of your vulnerability issues as person, not actor, must be for you to deal with. Your personal self can choose to remain invulnerable. However, your professional and character self must be able to access such emotion. You may also discover that addressing such roadblocks in your acting will lead you to further self-exploration—perhaps through some of the readings suggested in this chapter or through your own research—and that is to be encouraged. Finally, as always, approach all your roadblocks with great self-awareness, and should the work feel overwhelming, discontinue until a later time or seek counsel from a professional.

Dr. Jason Moser suggests a common approach to all the possibilities contained within this chapter. He suggests keeping a diary of when the issue occurs and logging that information to be reviewed later:

I ask people to keep a log of their personal lives, as well as their professional lives, for self-monitoring, which is basically keeping a journal or diary. So you have to commit yourself to raising awareness of your own ways of being and trying to put it under the microscope at least for a week. Give yourself a week and say, "Okay, this week I'm going to figure out whatever." Keep tabs of all those times you feel yourself holding something back from somebody else from an interpersonal exchange. So it's always about somebody else, so as you're going throughout your week, note the time, date, what was going on, your feelings at that time, and what you did. Try to raise more awareness, "Okay, what did I just hold back and who is that with?" "What was happening in my day otherwise that might have led up to that event?" You want to get more insight because you don't quite get it yet. You have to look at it more closely, kind of the ABCs of it—the anxiety, behavior, and consequence. Keep a daily log of that, it's really informative and then you get the whole picture after that week and can think, "Okay, I'm starting to see some patterns" because you will see patterns, and even if you don't see it the first time, you keep at it, patterns will emerge. Things like fear anxiety, and avoidance and difficulty in trust are not random. The more you look at them, the more something will pop out at you.

The chapter shares the most common roadblocks for actors. The roadblocks affect both the internally based and externally based actor. The external actor who has crippling self-doubt may find some of the internal strategies useful. But as noted, every actor has an individual pathway and therefore individual roadblocks. So, if you find your issue is not explored here, investigate through further research and self-reflection and adapt some of the strategies offered in this book to address your personal roadblock. Use concepts related to common and similar roadblocks to assist with your personal struggle. As always, the goal is to find your personal bridge to unencumbered acting.

## Anxiety

Anxiety in any form is an overstimulation of the brain that obfuscates the natural functions of any human. For an actor, anxiety can manifest itself as stage fright. Certainly anxiety and fear are natural responses when sharing your work in front of hundreds of people. Anxiety in performance is expected and can positively affect the actor to a state of relaxed readiness, where you are present enough to accept any new challenge thrown to you while acting, yet calm enough to perform your duties as actor.

Dr. Chris Hopwood explains the unique relationship between actors and anxiety: "My sense is that this is evolutionary, and that performing is a situation that we are not prepared for. Generally being the focus of a lot of people's attention isn't usually a good thing. It usually means something bad is about to happen, so my guess is that it's more of an evolutionary, unnatural, scary situation to be in, which is universal." The mere profession of acting is, by nature, an invitation to anxiety. Hopwood continues:

> Everybody has a hard time with public speaking; I have given hundreds of talks, I am not an actor, but I have been on stage lots and lots of times, and invariably, you get a little nervous just before you give a talk. This is a human universal given the fact that nothing about natural selection prepared us to be in that situation. Again, my sense is that actors are so brave that they can think, "It doesn't matter to me" to maybe lessen the anxiety.

Putting yourself in situations where you are constantly on display is naturally anxiety inducing, and accepting Hopwood's assertion that actors are brave and unique can offer some salve to the actor's relationship to anxiety.

Anxiety is a roadblock when it is crippling or diminishes the work. This may manifest itself in an actor who, when rehearsing their work alone is free and confident, but when sharing their work in the classroom becomes paralyzed with fear which causes a retreat from their best possible work. There is also a mental taxation that comes from living on the various planes as self, actor, and character that can heighten an actor's connection to anxiety. At times, the juggling of these three planes makes an actor highly affected by and attuned to the anxious state of performance. Anxiety can pitch a performance to a high frequency where the performer's lack of ease makes both performer and audience uncomfortable.

Anxiety does not mean anything until you prescribe a personal meaning to this general form and examine its relation to you. Moser urges the actor to examine anxiety in two specific areas: emotion and thought. He explains:

> One of the main focuses of my work is anxiety. Specifically, how anxiety gets in the way of people performing, mostly from an

academic setting, but really in life, and how it interferes function-ally more broadly in any walk of life whether its work, class, or rela-tionships. It focuses primarily on two ways that anxiety can get in the way of managing emotions. Whether they are anxious emotions themselves, that's obvious. Anxious people have to focus on manag-ing anxiety. But other emotions are involved too—anger, depression, sadness, and even happiness. Some people with anxiety have a hard time experiencing positive emotion because it's scary; it can lead to bad emotions. Going from happy to bad or happy to sad or happy to anxious feels worse than being slightly anxious all the time.

While it may appear that an actor's anxiety would be housed in the emotional categorization, since actors must rely on their emotional capacity, the second area may be more common for actors deeply affected by anxiety. Moser continues:

> The other kind of mechanism or avenue is people's cognition: what people pay attention to, what people think; so anxious people have particular ways of thinking: bad things happening; symptoms in their bodies, meaning that they are going to die or have a heart attack. They also pay more attention to threatening things in their own selves like anxious thoughts or anxious feelings, as well as pref-erentially paying attention to negative elements in the environment.

By dividing anxiety into separate areas, the actor may be better able to classify and quantify its effect. So, if anxiety makes you frustrated, depressed, and hopeless, you may better manage it because you feel those emotions coming on. Similarly, if you have an unhealthy pattern of thinking that includes constant self-flagellation in anxious situa-tions, you may better train yourself to overcome such thoughts because you are aware of their patterns.

As mentioned in the previous section, the most recognizable anxi-ety in actors is stage fright—it's even named for our profession. Unless the causes and effects are clarified, stage fright can remain generalized. Fear of being in front of an audience, social anxiety, or performance anxiety—your personal relationship with this overall concept needs closer examination. The fear at the moment of performance, despite the hours of rehearsal or your ownership of the role, does little to assuage the anxiety roadblocks in your professional life. Stage fright can also bleed into your personal self in the form of social anxiety. Most intro-verted actors are asked to "perform" off stage as well as on. Networking events or breaks from rehearsal are two situations when the introverted actor can become anxious. Social anxiety can easily be transferred to performance, unless there is great care in managing it while plying your craft. Finally, the dread of the actual performance and the overwhelm-ing fear of failure can be traced to performance anxiety. Combinations of these various actor-related anxieties can define your relationship with this roadblock.

Hopwood notes a way to lessen all types of anxiety through the rep-etition of performance:

> The way we understand anxiety is a combination of classical condi-tioning and negative reinforcement. The classical conditioning part is a stimulus paired with an anxiety response, so for whatever reason, you learn that spiders are scary or public speaking is scary. And again, I don't think you have to learn that; I think people are born thinking that being on stage in front of lots of people all looking at you is a scary thing.

So, the normal reaction to such fears is avoidance and that avoidance is the roadblock. Hopwood continues, "once that classical condition-ing response is there, the negative reinforcement part is; therefore, I avoid ever being in that situation; I avoid seeing spiders, I avoid driving because cars are scary, or I avoid airplanes because flying is scary, or I avoid being in the situation of public speaking, or acting, or any situa-tion where there's going to be a lot of eyes on me." Hopwood also offers a rather direct solution to this anxiety: "The treatment is quite straight-forward. You make the person do the thing they are afraid of—over and over and over again. And the idea is that eventually, if you can get to the avoidance behavior, you can break the fear response." For an actor, that means a continual immersion and repetition in performance. This can easily be transferred to the actual repetition of auditioning or the long run of a show.

Some reinterpret anxiety as a motivator. Stage fright can be a way to get the thrill that adrenaline gives you. Actors can be adrenaline junkies. Sometimes the body responds positively, and therefore, the roadblock could be the addiction to it. Neuroscience supports this. The physical sensations can be exciting, but it can also offer clues as to where to focus your attention in eradicating your roadblock. Marika Reisberg points out:

> Anxiety generates sensations. When on the path to anxiety, an awareness of how and where the first anxiety body cue happens can assist you to answer the anxiety experience and offer a solution to how you stop it. When you give anxiety a concentrated focus, it may get bigger for some, and it reduces for others. Either way, you have awareness that something is happening in your body, in this instance of the sensation of anxiety; you have the option to do something.

She offers some options related to these discoveries: "You might allow yourself to feel it, you might distract yourself, you might try a breathing technique, or you might choose to do nothing. Whatever you do in that moment is your choice to change or not." One way to overcome this roadblock is an examination of its cues and physical manifestations.

Examine your three selves and see if your personal anxiety also negatively affects your professional and character selves. Do all of your interactions in all three areas carry the same amount and type of anxiety? If the answer is yes, then personal anxiety must be managed so you can do your job more effectively.

### Questions to Consider

What are the moments as an actor that make me most anxious?
Why does this anxiety happen when performing?
How does it manifest itself in my characters?
What safety behaviors do I employ?
Do I enjoy the anxiety?
What would I need to do in order to get rid of the anxiety?

### Strategies

A great place to begin is by acknowledging that all other actors have similar anxieties. Your work is to distinguish your personal relationship with anxiety. There is a difference between self-based anxieties and character-based anxieties, and that can be made clearer by trying to establish a professional persona that comprehends your work is harmed by an overanxious state. Your character probably does not have the same anxiety that you do. Your personal relationship with anxiety intersects the three selves and is impinging your work in unwelcome ways. Understanding this with a clear delineation may reduce the roadblock.

Marika Reisberg suggests trying breathing or visualization techniques or distractions. She suggests, "Four square breathing [also known as box breathing] or visualizing thoughts of anxiety on a conveyer belt to see them move away. Immerse yourself in another activity. These are ways to de-escalate the problem." Breathing can alleviate anxiety, if it is the right kind of breathing. Focusing on the exhalation and blowing out breath as you would with a bubble wand were also suggested.

Setting goals in rehearsal and performance in relation to anxiety are suggested. These include investing more deeply in the performance, by focusing solely on your partner and the given circumstance of the script. A clearer understanding of why the audience is there (not to judge but to be entertained) may also help to release high anxiety in performance.

Other suggestions include journaling in the third person to examine anxiety. As part of this journaling, create a list ranging from what makes you most anxious to least anxious and then carry out limited, guided exposure. Start small and build up your exposure to the events that cause you the most stress. For example, if auditions are currently fear-based, set the goal that when entering the room, you try for genuine openness when greeting the auditors and build from there. Similarly to building up through exposure, share your fears of anxiety in performance with an ever-widening circle of confidantes. Share your fears with one friend, then peers, and then your director. By having to explain the issue to many, it may dissipate.

*Supplementary Reading*

It is with anxiety, specifically, that neurosciences such as neuroimaging can offer a deeper understanding of the physiology related to your brain and your roadblock. Look at anxiety and peak performance studies in cognitive and behavioral neuroscience as a way to examine anxiety from various vantage points. The scientific understanding of limit systems in neuropsychology, a system that shoots adrenaline and cortisol into your brain when you are anxious, may offer relief to the actor so focused on emotion. By studying the natural functions of the brain, the irrational fears of the actor may be dampened.

The work of Dr. David M. Clark and the examination of where anxiety comes from can assist in understanding your relationship with it. His work was offered by the consultants as a place to begin further study. Also important for the actor are several books by Dr. Todd Kashdan who examines the power of negative emotions. Similar to the way in which third-person self-talk is a way to remove worry from self-evaluation, the work of Gerardo Ramirez and Sian L. Beilock concern how writing about test worries can actually improve achievement in the classroom may be helpful.

## Body Awareness

Actors are on display. The camera captures their physical presence. The proscenium frames their bodies so they can be better observed. Their headshot is their calling card. The actor's physical form and the actor's self are one and the same. This realization makes Moser assert that, "Actors are brave."

To cover the title of this section in its entirety is too broad a subject matter for the scope of this book and therefore this section only introduces the multiplicity of topics. So, use the main observations and questions to guide you to the best bridge for your specific roadblock. As Moser notes, some of the issues that may be connected to body awareness are possibly "deep core issues that need to be recommended by a trained expert. I would have to guess that shame or family could be connected, and that is too deep to explore in an acting class." He confirms that the external and physical actor can be impeded by an internal issue. As with all the possible roots of the roadblocks in your work, you must decide when and what to explore in relation to your barrier.

For the purposes of this book, body awareness can fall into two major categories; lack of a physical connection—actors unable to commit to physical choices; and body image—actors who have impasses related to their physical appearance. Although they can be linked, they may also be separate issues that require separate attention.

The first category involves actors who may lack the internal wiring that allows them to connect and transform their body physically. This may be a lack of understanding in relation to controlling the anatomy (like a person who lacks the current coordination to have flexibility of form) or it may be a more ingrained roadblock. The most common is a reliance on the internal as a means to avoid the external. Actors who suffer from this roadblock find no connection between their head and body. They act from their head and understand the character but lack the requisite outlet to physically release their analysis. This is one of the most obvious of all roadblocks because the body remains unengaged, as the actor is stranded internally. Marika Reisberg suggests another path this sort of roadblock may take: "When we lose a connection to our bodies, we can fall into habitual automatic pilot movements where we have mastered the appearance of being embodied to fool others. Because as soon as we are allowed to not be present in our work or disconnect from our body experience, we will. The draw to disengage is powerful."

The second category concerns the natural propensity of actors to compare themselves to others. In this highly competitive business, competition engenders such comparison. This natural extension of the business enhances an already fragile personal self's awareness of body. Moser notes, "Anxiety is always going to be there and actors have several options. You have the option of going to the gym or getting plastic surgery if you deeply, honestly think your beauty is costing you your job." Better energy may be spent in examining your values related to this issue. He continues, "A deeper place to consider is what you place importance on. Do you value the beautiful or do you value the authentic?"

Moser's use of the word "authentic" has resonance for many actors. Your individuality is what makes your work unique. Your authenticity is what separates you from the rest, so great value in and cultivation of your authentic professional self and body is necessary. For some, that argument may reduce the roadblock related to body awareness; for others, it is an empty homily you have heard too often with little residual effect.

Perhaps your issue is not as closely or solely linked to comparison to others but rather to a deeper lack of respect for self. In more minor cases of this, a cultivation of a veneration of self can be attained through the standard strategies discussed throughout the book. Sometimes this issue may be more difficult to resolve. Roadblocks can lead to body dysmorphia, eating disorders, and other issues that usually point to the need for deeper focus outside of the studio with trained professionals.

## Questions to Consider

Are there self-imposed physical limitations to my work?
Am I willing to address them at this time?
Do I feel physically overwhelmed when acting?
Does this roadblock offer me more security at this point than I am willing to part with?
What do I need to feel physically free on stage?
What is my relationship to the audience?

## Strategies

The unique forms that this roadblock takes require unique approaches—more than can be covered here. As a general rule, Reisberg notes, "Mindfulness in relation to body acceptance can be difficult. The word 'acceptance' can be a hang-up. So try acknowledging the issue. That doesn't mean I have to like it or approve, but it is what it is. It is an acknowledgment. You can talk later about acceptance." Acknowledgement of the issue may allow you some freedom from the roadblock's stranglehold.

More than likely, the physical roadblock can be best discovered by physical clues. Doing a body scan may yield results. Reisberg asks you to begin noticing physical clues in order to best find ways to bridge your work. Here she explains how she will work with her patients who have limited physical awareness: "I want to focus in on what's confusing for them. I'm trying to identify it. I'm not trying to make sense of it. But I want you to focus on what your body is trying to tell you. Not necessarily put a story to it. So how do you then move your body in a way that activates that?" Reisberg understands that not all actors can be so physically self-aware. She continues, "If they're not comfortable moving, we don't move. We do a lot of talking. Or, we talk about what movement is. Breathing is movement. We're constantly breathing, so we start with breath and build from there. I start where there is a level of comfort to help them gain a physical connection." Deciding on what level of physical work you are willing to do is important. You can set the boundaries (like the patient in Reisberg's example) of what you are comfortable with.

For an actor, being embodied, open, and receptive to your scene partner requires physical freedom. The first type of physical road-block requires you to gain more understanding and control of your body; that can usually be bridged through repetition, exercise, and a strong concentration on physical adeptness. Usually accompanying this strategy are many moments of frustration related to the time, practice, and setbacks required to create a better physical connection. But the connection between coordination and confidence can be gained.

Reisberg offers a few exercises to assist with body awareness: "Moving body scans are a great way to start feeling your body. Starting at your feet, sequentially move up your body to your head, slowly moving each section: feet, ankles, lower legs, knees, upper legs, hips, pelvis, and so on. By bringing awareness and attention to your body in this fashion, you are able to notice where you're hold-ing tension, pain, ease, lightness and breath." Taking stock of your physical as well as mental clues is key. She continues, "Once you have systematically brought attention and awareness to your body, the next step is to engage with your scene partner while maintaining your connection to your body. This is easier said than done and can require practice."

Physical activity is key in this work of overcoming a lack of con-nection to the body. It can also be fun, as Reisberg points out in the following suggestion: "A living room or dorm room solo dance party is a great way to connect with your body. Allowing your body and not your mind to lead the movements not only gives your mind a rest, but it offers your body the opportunity to cycle stress, tension, and other body-stifling things to transform. In the beginning, this may be easier said than done, so, as mentioned previously, this is a prac-tice, something to be done more than once." The idea of repetition is important while remembering to not be discouraged about current limitations.

Overcoming the second type of physical roadblock related to comparison or self-image remains difficult for an actor who is focused on how they look to others or themselves. So, in a scene that requires you to feel attractive, sexually liberated, physically unrestrained, or demonstrate other aspects of the role that make you physically uncomfortable, the goal is to reduce the focus from your personal self on your self-image or the audience and amplify the focus of your acting self to your scene partner. Adjusting the percentages of attention may offer you some freedom from the unwanted self-focus, as described by the actor in Chapter 5. To be an embodied actor requires a full physical trust and immersion in the concept of listening and responding with your whole self—not just selected parts.

Other strategies include motivational interviewing where the client is focused on goal-oriented results—in this case, related to acceptance of their current physical form. Questions may be asked such as "Is your current self-image helpful to your work?" Another strategy is retraining unproductive repetitive thoughts to a more positive and productive way of thinking. So, rather than the unending inner monologue of "I hate my body," perhaps reposition that negative thinking to, "What can I do to make a change?," if change is what you want. Or perhaps the easier, "I acknowledge this is where I am right now" can be a better entrance into retraining your brain. You can begin to seek real options rather than repeating the cycle you wish to end. The overall goal, as Reisberg reminds you, is "acknowledgement. Once you have an awareness of what is happening, you then have the option and ability to change it."

### Supplementary Reading

There is much written about self-image and body awareness that is easily transferrable to the actor. Since this roadblock takes on so many forms, it is suggested that you consult with a health care professional to best address your specific area of concern.

Knowing your physical body can be extremely helpful, so picking up an anatomy coloring-in book is a great way to learn about your physical body, while also offering the chance to unwind and offer a distraction through coloring. One well-known suggestion is *The Anatomy Coloring Book* by Wynn Kapit and Lawrence Elson. Additionally, Bonnie Bainbridge Cohen, the founder of Body-Mind Centering® offers incredible exercises and information in her book *Sensing, Feeling, and Action: The Experiential Anatomy of Body-Mind Centering* on ways to experience each body system separately as well as a whole.

## Emotion

Actors are expected to be able to replicate truthful human emotions, summon up passion, and play scenes of high stakes with life and death situations. Why then do some actors suffer from a roadblock of a fear of emotion? This fear usually manifests itself by reducing what should be the highly charged emotions called for by the dramatic situation in the script to a place that is comfortable for the actor. The notes these actors usually receive include "I need more"; "You are underplaying"; "Share your work with the audience." All those notes may be code for, "Your roadblock is a fear of emotion."

How that roadblock developed can be down to several possibilities. Marika Reisberg suggests it may have been caused by

> punishment [a time out for crying], shame [boys don't cry], a gender component [girls shouldn't be loud], or cultural stigmas [we don't yell] related to emotion. It may also come from a societal stigma related to familial issues, where a family may say or model that emotions aren't good. In actuality, emotions aren't good or bad; they just are. It is how we behave with them that offers a lasting impression.

This last part of the quote is key to embracing the idea of creating a large emotional life on stage or on camera. How you interact with emotion is an important part of your professional self. Within the three selves, an odd relationship with emotions exists. You spend your personal life trying to manage and diminish your emotions, but then your professional life requires you to summon up deep unrestricted access to all emotions. The highly emotional journey of any good character is what great writers dramatize, and what excites the audience and exhausts the actor.

It only makes sense that you might currently have greater access to a limited number of emotions because you have more experience with some than others. You prefer sharing those to which you have easier access. Some are more fun to play, and more fun to feel. Your attention should be focused on those emotions that offer you more resistance in terms of accessing them. Moser offers a broader perspective related to actor and emotion: "Often, [actors] are dealing with those emotions that are really hard to bring out and amplify because they are negative emotions. Those may be the hardest to do; maybe it's anger, grief, depression, sadness, or anxiety." This is the most common aspect for actors. However, Moser notes, "Maybe for some of you it's really hard to bring out positive emotions. And the state of the research really has to do with how we understand emotional experience and the decrease of negative emotion." Most research currently is not related to the actor's unique plight. For some studies that do address this area, I refer you to the work by Dr. Thalia M. Goldstein and Dr. Paul Bloom, who have begun to examine why psychologists should study actors.

So, if you have a roadblock with emotion, Moser reminds you of the unique job that actors have chosen as their profession, and as such, there is little research to assist you in your struggle: "The research now has a lot to do with dampening things; we want to understand how to dampen negative experiences and negative emotions. We also want to understand how to dampen positive emotions for people who have bipolar or manic depression." The actor's goal of accessing both positive and negative emotions mostly exists outside such study. For the actor with this roadblock, being able to label and understand those emotions that you consider "negative" or "positive" is important. It can usually assist you in identifying which emotional sticking points exist.

Another reason for the categorization is purely professional, related to the analysis and understanding of certain characters and their relationship to emotion. Moser explains, "One kind of clinical parallel to what [actors] want to be able to portray are psychopaths. Psychopaths don't feel enough negative emotion, so we think, 'Oh let me get you to practice feeling more negative emotion because that's what you need to do to develop empathy.'" Being able to label, manage, and access all the emotions necessary for a variety of roles makes an actor more marketable. By avoiding the emotional needs of the character, you limit the opportunity for jobs.

### Questions to Consider

Am I satisfied with a limited emotional range?
What is it that scares me most about showing emotion as an actor?
What is it about accessing these emotions as an actor that scares me?
What emotions do I like to play on stage?
What are the emotional performances I respond to?
If I take a risk emotionally when I perform, what happens?

*Strategies*

Moser notes that the most positive strategy is to "think of emotion as a tool rather than an extension of who you are. Think of emotion as an experience where you allow yourself to be free to do whatever is needed without repercussions." Granting yourself permission to express these emotions that you have been otherwise told to avoid can come easier when you also remember that it is the character shouting, crying, or screaming, and not you. Separation of personal self from these negative emotions is imperative.

You must begin to normalize the idea of emotion in your professional life by examining whether or not it is the fear of emotion in you (personally) or the fear of somebody else's emotions (character). If you are able to let the character experience those feelings while you remain personally mindful of "her" actions, you may be able to access the required emotion. If you insist that you "aren't an angry person," that may always remain true, even while you portray someone who lives in an emotional state of anger.

Some other possible strategies include examining the "What if?" or the "downward arrow technique" (described in Chapter 6), starting with "What if you fully embraced the emotion?" and working through until you get to the root of the issue. You may find that the root is that your fear of emotion may come from a panicked idea that, by opening up this pathway, you might have a psychotic break from reality. Such isolated incidents (sometimes urban legend) should not be an excuse to avoid fully exploring your craft. Mind-altering substances that promote a paranoid state and aggravate the "break" usually account for an actor who loses his personal self in a role.

Scaffolding to high emotion is another strategy. You may wish to explore slowly, raising the stakes in each pass of a scene or monologue. If you start out with your comfort zone, how can you raise the stakes each time to get to the level you want? Similarly, gauge your emotional intensity on a numeric scale so that this next run will be a "seven out of ten" in emotional intensity. The fear of emotion involves many layers and levels, and it is for you to identify the issues that most deeply affect your roadblock. Only you can answer what you fear when it comes to emotion. Dr. Chris Hopwood notes, "As an actor, you must learn to be okay with negative emotions. With a focus on being aware, accepting, and tolerant of emotion."

Moser relates an exercise used commonly in his lab that involves emotion-inducing pictures to gain skills with emotional accessibility: "We do these experiments in the lab, and we have people come in to look at pictures. There are huge databases of pictures that elicit reliably negative, arousing emotions, and we tell people to look at these things in order to examine their emotions." He suggests an adaptation for the actor: "You might view emotional images on your computer. Practicing viewing the image to elicit the emotion you need may be another useful way to be able to amplify these things so you can better understand emotional difference and flexibility." Using these images, music, or readings can elicit a strong emotional response and allow you to enter the scene in a heightened state, more able to access the requisite emotions.

From the physical therapy point of view, Reisberg reminds us that emotions show up in different parts of the body. She notes,

> [Emotions] also have different body postures and facial expressions associated with them. There are ways you can explore emotions in your physical body that may offer some a way to connect to them easier. For example, thinking about fear/anxiety, there are physiological changes that happen in your body, you can freeze, faint, fly (run away) or fight; explore how these feel in your body when your body "freezes in fear."

By separating the emotion from negative thought and examining it physically, the roadblock may become less overwhelming. Reisberg continues, "Having a body understanding of emotions may help an actor express them more authentically without necessarily losing themselves in the emotion."

### Supplementary Reading

Look at the work of Steven Hayes and others on Experiential Avoidance to see how the cost of avoiding emotions has further ramifications. This is closely linked to ACT, introduced in Chapter 4. You may also want to look at writings about the Imposter Syndrome that examines how some individuals currently lack the ability for the internalization of accomplishments. Readings about "The Gift of Love Theory" and works by Dr. Lorna Smith Benjamin may also prove useful.

## Extroversion/introversion

Extroversion and introversion are not roadblocks; they are categorizations created by Carl Jung that often impact how an actor can deal with roadblocks. These two personality types impact the way in which an actor communicates with all three selves, color interactions with others surrounding performance, and inform your approach to the craft. The inclusion of extroversion and introversion offers ways to augment strategies related to the other topics covered in this chapter.

As stated throughout, each actor has a personal journey and approach to acting. The spectrum of possible pathways to defining an individual process is heavily influenced by the type of person you are. The extroverted actor may align more closely with the improvisation and the immediacy of the teachings of Sanford Meisner. The introverted actor may relate to the use of inner monologue and the reliance on given circumstances of Stella Adler. As Marika Reisberg notes, for extroverted and introverted actors, "One isn't better than the other. What does matter is what is sustainable in either case. How much does the actor give away or get exhausted in either approach?"

The examination of these classifications and the understanding of their general patterns may allow actors to create characters that "live" in their opposing categorization. How successful can an extroverted actor be at portraying the need for solitude of the introverted character? Or how fully does the introvert have the ability to portray a character who thrives on interaction? All actors have the ability to understand and empathize with the other categorization, and most do have some level of both, an ambivert, within them. For some actors though, those assignments in portraying a character so opposite to your innate being are emotionally draining. The mixture of character qualities and personal inclination may be at odds.

The professional self of the actor is also highly influenced by this classification in relation to auditions, networking, and downtime in a rehearsal. In these moments, the professional and personal self may be at war. The introvert who wants time alone or the extrovert who seeks others can impact the dynamic of any class or production. Throughout all professional arenas, the needs of the individual (related to the three selves) require cultivation. The extroverted and introverted actor were covered in assessments, testimonials, and several sections in the book, but a deeper examination of theatrical practices could assist both actors and educators to find the best way to both disseminate and assimilate the information. Specific strategies may need to be employed.

## Questions to Consider

How does my introversion or extroversion affect my approach to acting?
Can I succeed using strategies that I would normally shy away from?
Am I able to cultivate a professional self that is more ambivert in nature?
Does my reaction to an actor in a different category impact my work with them?
Are there times when my introversion or extroversion overwhelms my work?
Are my characters portrayed honestly if they fall into a category other than my personal self?

## Strategies

The hope in any classroom is to allow both extroverts and introverts to learn and interact harmoniously, but that can be a challenge. Almost any exercise can excite one actor or panic another. Understanding the way in which you learn best (as in the testimonial in Chapter 5 from the introverted actor who needs time to process notes) can alleviate personal anxiety.

Reisberg understands the need for a blended classroom structure related to introverts and extroverts. She notes:

The idea of arousal and how it relates to introverts and extroverts is an important awareness. Being able to de-escalate your system to manage your level of arousal following a particularly emotional scene for introverts (personally) or extroverts (professionally), there are particular body movements that have been shown to help re-set your system. They come from Brain Gym and are quick, easy body postures that have maximum effect on supporting a return to an internal baseline. The Carla Hannaford book *Smart Moves: Why Learning is Not All in Your Head* is a great place to learn these techniques.

The use of physical centering techniques following emotional work may be important for both introverts and extroverts.

Extroversion and introversion are not choices, but innate personality components, so both actor and educator should begin to adapt the best process to reach the individual categorization. Dr. Jason Moser provides some accepted basic characteristics below of the introvert and extrovert, which I have adapted and augmented for the actor:

Extroverts can better succeed in very public leadership roles while introverts may feel more comfortable with ensemble work. This does not mean that introverts do not make great leaders, but an introvert in a leadership role may be best assigned if there is planning rather than immediate results needed. It also does not mean that extroverts cannot merge within an ensemble without usurping attention. These same caveats apply to the statements below.

At times, extroverts are better able to reflect on an exercise immediately and vocally, while an introvert may succeed through private reflection and journaling.

Extroverts gain energy from being around groups of people, while an introvert might feel overwhelmed by the situation. So in class and rehearsals and during breaks, managing the time of either category is important.

Extroverts may have to offer verbal response to your critique, while an introvert may take time away from class to process.

The extrovert will most likely succeed in exercises that require boldness, while the introvert will shine in exercises of analysis.

Extroverts prefer to get up and try something immediately to see how it works, while introverts may need to take time to analyze it from various angles.

These basic principles can best guide you in how you can achieve better results. For educators, it is important to find a blend of these exercises to reach all learning styles. So, while you may regard improvisation with reverence, others may regard it with fear. And so it goes for all the methods we adopt when we approach acting. The goal is to reach the student in the most productively personal way possible.

As mentioned earlier in this book, Susan Cain's TED Talks and her writings, including *Quiet: The Power of Introverts,* offer deep and rich examples of how society has been created with extroversion at its core. Her work is important for understanding the way in which actors perform and teachers teach.

# Hiding

What does hiding mean to an actor when you make a living through exposure? For an actor, hiding can be divided into two categories. The first category is hiding through tricks—such as humor, wild choices, and great technique. The second is hiding through limitations—like not allowing yourself to look foolish, or presenting only the best version of yourself. In both cases, hiding restricts the humanity of your character by funneling edited choices to the character self. An actor who hides puts too many limits on her work.

In the first category, the actor who hides behind tricks may have a great reliance on animated voices or extreme physicality, and while this may have the appearance of bravery and freedom, it may actually be a way for the actor to hide. If these multiple characters lack honesty, then an examination of a roadblock related to the personal self is necessary. The best character actors are able to make extreme transformations while also retaining and displaying a humanity and depth from a personal connection.

Another category is the actor who relies on great diction, confident stances, and perfectly executed choices may be using technique as a way to avoid the honesty necessary for great acting. The technically proficient actor, while commendable, may be using their aptitude and prowess as a way to distract from a disturbing lack of internal connection. The goal as actor seems to be to gain admiration rather than empathy from the audience.

In the second category, an actor who hides as a means to avoid looking foolish (like the actor discussed in Chapter 1) avoids all emotions, situations, and characteristics deemed foolish in others. This limited view of the world uses an unhealthy dose of the personal self to overtake the actor self. Only the type of character your personal self believes is appropriate will be allowed on stage. You may feel that the script asks you to do ridiculous things or react in ways that are not how people react. While that occasionally may be true, if that excuse continues, it is a pattern. And if it is a pattern, it is a roadblock.

The final category related to hiding means creating characters that have no negative or ulterior motives. You present only the most sanitized, acceptable, and audience-pleasing version of the character, and by extension, of yourself. Dr. Jason Moser notes that results in "putting only your best self on stage," and presenting "only [the] emotions you have processed, vetted, and find acceptable."

Moser's statement may be true for all types of actors who have roadblocks related to hiding. Whether hiding is based on extreme, technical, safe, or sanitized choices, the actor is limiting the opportunity for a range of experiences. By acting in a zone of safety that allows you to hide, subtlety, messiness, danger, and grit may be missing from your work.

An examination of the motivation for a reliance on hiding may take you to other parts of the chapter, including self-esteem, emotion, or vulnerability. Or you may discover that hiding provides safety while performing. No matter the case, it is up to you to examine whether or not you wish to continue hiding or seek access to expanded choices.

### Questions to Consider

Which of the four types of "hiding" actor am I, if any?
Can I recognize when other actors are hiding?
Do I need hiding in order to cope with the pressure of being on stage?
If I come out of hiding while performing what will happen?
Am I relying on hiding in my acting for a reason?
What kind of choices could I make if I was not hiding?

### Strategies

Hiding in one of the bravest of professions—acting—is understandable. It is also unwelcome. How the actor bridges their craft to allow them a fuller range may take many forms. There are mixed messages related to your work. Examine the positive attention you have received for hiding. For extreme choices, you are called "bold." For technical work, you are called "clean." For safe choices, you are called "consistent." For edited choices, you are called "likeable." All are fine adjectives for any actor. But positive reinforcement can do damage to an actor at times, if those affirmative descriptions become all your work is about. You may want to explore opposites when approaching future roles and auditions. Set goals related to rehearsals and explore those underutilized areas. Recalibrate your analysis to address these issues head on and make choices that surprise or scare you. Allow a fuller emotional experience on stage. People are complicated, and to avoid those complications means you diminish your work as actor.

Dr. Chris Hopwood suggests mentalization observation as a way to gain understanding and empathy for complicated characters. By thinking like others through observation you can gain empathy in your work that will allow a broader range of character traits. Mentalization observation is an exercise that can be done any time there is another person around. Go to a park and observe a stranger. Watch how they interact with the world, and begin to supply their inner monologue as you observe. You will begin to transform your thoughts to that of another and expand your range.

"Opportunities to exaggerate the hiding or physicalizing the hiding are ways to learn more about it," posits Marika Reisberg. She suggests, "Paying attention to your internal body landscape when engaging in hiding could offer more information to the actor about why it is happening, or it may highlight the wisdom in it." She also recommends a mindfulness exercise called "One eye in, One eye out" that trains attention:

> You start with sending all your attention outside yourself, looking at the room you are in, the colors shapes, words, smells, sounds. Next, sending all your attention inside yourself, noticing your breathing, your heart beat, your body sensations. Next, you send "one eye in and one eye out" where you are simultaneously paying attention to the space/environment you are in as well as your internal body experience. Again, training your attention to go where you want it is something to practice.

Reisberg suggests asking, "What is the wisdom in hiding?" Does it have the opposite effect, so often covered in this book, where the roadblock draws attention to itself despite your best efforts? She continues, "The real question is, 'Why are you hiding?'" This question can only be answered personally, and more than likely, the answer may lead to other roadblocks.

### Supplementary Reading

Once you have answered the above question posed by Reisberg, you may be directed to another section of the chapter. The answer may be that you hide because you have a fear of emotion, issues related to vulnerability, dread of judgment, or many other common roadblocks. You may discover that hiding is really a symptom of a roadblock.

Reisberg also offers the following: "There are so many books out there about getting to know yourself. As an artist, I think a great one is *The Artist's Way* by Julia Cameron. The abundance of exercises in Cameron's book can be carried out for all three selves. Another book I recommend is *Trust the Process: An Artist's Guide to Letting Go* by Shaun McNiff."

## Intimacy

Intimacy is one of those rare things only an actor is called upon to summon with a complete stranger. How can you be open enough to create an appearance of immediate intimacy with someone you just met? How do you create a performance that allows for intimacy with someone who you don't necessarily like off stage? How can you lack intimacy as your personal self, yet project intimacy within a scene? You act.

Intimacy takes on many forms. Intimacy can be related to distance—how close your partner is to you. It can be interpersonal—scenes that require actors to dramatize what in real life are considered intimate moments. Or they can be based on the subject matter—scenes that contain sexual or other topics whose honest approach requires a deeply particular connection. This strange actor phenomenon of instant chemistry and requisite intimacy is actually the subject of several workshops (most notably those run by Tonia Sina) covering how to safely manufacture intimacy when dealing with sexuality and violence on the stage. At these workshops, the facilitator works with actors and directors to assist in creating an atmosphere of safety and trust.

A lack of intimacy can manifest itself in an actor who gazes just above your partner's eyes in order to not allow your partner look at you intimately. This common safety behavior does not deliver the actor's intended appearance but actually draws attention to the issue (as most do). So while you may want to present the appearance of being intimate and looking in her eyes, your scene partner and the audience all know the truth—you have a roadblock with intimacy. The same is true of other safety behaviors related to intimacy, such as laughing when a moment makes you uncomfortable or fidgeting in order to distract yourself from a true connection.

Marika Reisberg suggests, "Intimacy is hard to have with someone else if you don't have it with yourself. Most people's rules with intimacy are implicit and explicit. And there is a gender difference. What men and women each see as intimate is very different. But everyone's interpretation is different." It is suggested that, with this roadblock, as with the others discussed in the chapter, you define "intimacy" for yourself. What is intimacy? You may be able to talk about any intimate subject frankly, but when it comes to actually being intimate with your partner on stage, you seize up. The inverse may be true as well. So defining intimacy in relation to your roadblock is imperative.

Intimacy is highly connected to vulnerability and trust. Both are needed to access the intimacy required. In order to create a space where intimacy can be performed, intimacy needs to be addressed and prepared for by director or teacher when working on such material. Security (including the rehearsal environment) is of the utmost necessity.

### Questions to Consider

Do I recognize intimacy in myself at all when acting?
What does it look like when others are acting in an intimate fashion?
Is keeping myself safe from intimacy more important than achieving it?
Why is intimacy important for an actor?
As an actor what are my boundaries with intimacy?
Can I achieve intimacy?

### Strategies

Luckily, Marika Reisberg avows, "Lack of intimacy can be relearned as actor. It is a re-enacted pattern in other areas of your lives. The goal for the actor is to change those patterns. Communication with yourself, your partner, and your director is the key." It is through open and honest communication that you can gain the trust and vulnerability necessary to achieve true intimacy on stage.

This above paragraph seems to suggest that, in order to be a good actor, you must give away your whole personal self to achieve this elusive goal. This is not the case. Being intimate requires a parceling up of feelings that you can feel comfortable with. If you have moral boundaries linked to sexual topics, or physical boundaries related to personal beliefs, these are to be respected and upheld. Similarly, you are not required to be in love with your partner in order to play that relationship honestly. You retain your personal truth but access the feelings surrounding intimacy.

Reisberg explains a successful strategy used in therapy: "In a session I would say, 'Okay. So you're telling me about people who are invading your space.' The patient may say, 'I don't have enough personal space. How can I establish my space?' So then we exaggerate and physicalize this issue until she feels personally comfortable." A similar technique may be used for the actor. Reisberg continues, "She got to tell me where her personal space was. She kept telling me to go further and further away until I was across the room. You can feel that embodied experience of, 'Wow. For the first time in my life, I'm actually able to tell someone my personal space is you across the room.' And then I'd feel the stress decrease, not completely, but a little bit." This same boundary creation can also have similar success for the actor by creating or sharing internalized, recognizable limits. Having a clear set of rules with your partner and director or teacher is fundamental. This frame or contract offers boundaries for safety within this sort of exploration. In order to gain the desired result, disclosing the actor's fears as you approach the work may be a strategy, but that must also have limits. The individual with the roadblock sets the level of intimacy throughout the process.

The fear of rejection is what drives most intimacy issues, so it is important to create freedom in performance without that fear. Being able to trust that your scene partner will not reject you may create a bridge to intimacy. This may be achieved through carefully coached exercises. Using one of the basic safety behaviors related to intimacy—avoiding eye contact with your partner—there are a few strategies to employ. First, allow the scene to stop each time the safety behavior appears. If the partner notices the lack of eye contact, she may stop the scene and wait for you to re-engage. That simple awareness and con-tract between partners may begin to break the pattern.

Another strategy is to run the scene without words. By only using eye contact to perform the scene, you and your partner will be forced to establish a shared version of intimacy. This should not be an invitation for indication or pushed acting, but rather, an intimate performance of the scene, sans words, that may create a bond between the partners and allow access to intimacy.

Finally, warming up or preparing to shoot the scene should always begin with an honest check-in with the partner by looking deeply into his eyes. If you suffer from this safety behavior, you can eradicate it through daily focus. When having discussions as your personal self or as actor self, force yourself to maintain eye contact for more extended periods of time. You may then learn that if you lose eye contact for a bit, it can be easily re-engaged and rejection does not occur. These same pre-cepts can de adapted for any of the safety behaviors mentioned earlier. Through constant exercising to remove the safety behaviors in relation to a fear of rejection, the desired results with focus from the actor can be achieved.

Reisberg also suggests adapting a therapeutic technique for scene study called "Facing, Pacing, Spacing." She describes the exercise and its adaptation: "Most therapy happens face to face, and that can be incred-ibly intimidating for some, so what would it be like to be side to side with someone? As an actor, you might try an intimate scene standing or sitting next to your scene partner first, before moving face to face." She continues with another part of the exercise, similar to two of the exercises offered earlier in the book: "The pacing or speed of things can offer information as well, so you might try the scene in slow motion. The spacing piece is about your physical distance. This is something you can easily play with in a class, doing the exercise mentioned earlier where one person sets their physical boundary, and you do the scene at whatever distance that is." Reisberg has advice for the educator on how to handle this exercise: "After each trial, check in with the actors about what they noticed in their bodies doing each exercise and what information that might have given them. This might be difficult to do alone, but I think when working on intimacy with others, this would be a good place to start."

As with other strategies in this chapter, you may want to start by asking yourself, "What is the worst thing that could happen if I allow myself intimacy in this scene?" Similar to the downward arrow technique, keep asking yourself, "And if that happens, then what?" until you receive your answer. If the worst thing that could happen is completely out of the realm of possibility, you may gain a bit of comfort and trust related to your roadblock. Look over the answers given by the consultants related to this issue in the introduction of this book for other approaches.

Intimacy is one of the trickiest roadblocks because the boundaries and situations also place the educator in some dangerous territory. So as an actor, be cognizant of this concern and offer guidance and support to the educator to best assist you. In creating this reciprocal understanding, you can achieve success.

### Supplementary Reading

It is suggested that you consult other trust and vulnerability resources. The work of Foa and Kozak on Emotional Processing Theory, Gestalt psychology and Emotion Focused Therapy was also strongly suggested. Reisberg also suggests, "*The Creative Habit* by Twyla Tharp might be a great book for actors to use as a tool to experience intimacy. Again, it is a book filled with many exercises to help tap into creativity and could be done with all three selves to offer as deep an exploration as one chooses."

## Judgment

What makes good acting is based on subjective opinion. Unlike music, where a wrong note can be proven, actors must sometimes depend on the opinion of others to assist in guiding their work to success. These opinions are not fact-based, and conflicting feedback can derail an actor's natural instincts and confuse their ability to replicate truthful human behavior. This lack of rigid and definable boundaries of good and bad or right and wrong in acting incites confusion, which in turn, invites judgment. Many actors crumble or leave the business based on the roadblock of judgment. For the actor, judgment comes in three very important types.

Authoritarian judgment is seen as the ultimate power, where teachers, directors, producers, critics, and audience deem an actor's work as not worthy. The actor has surrendered autonomy to these leader figures and hangs precariously on their every word. Any note (however constructive) can send an actor with a judgment roadblock into a tailspin. Jonathon Novello notes, "The fear-based culture of the acting classroom can harm someone focused on authoritative judgment."

Peer judgment can be just as dangerous. An imagined lack of respect from or in comparison to the work of others can turn an otherwise secure actor into a mass of insecurities. As an actor with this issue, you are consumed with thoughts of comparison, jealousy, and hopelessness that you will ever be as good as others.

Perhaps the most difficult roadblock of all is self-judgment. In this roadblock, you as actor watch, critique, and disdain every "hollow" phrase you utter and every "false" move you make. It is this cycle of judgment that can entrap any actor to a point of suffocation. While a healthy amount of self-reflection is necessary to keep your work alive and growing, that reflection should most appropriately take place following the your actual performance and not within. Marika Reisberg notes, "In my experience talking to actors, it's that constant critic happening. 'I know where I need to go, but is someone going to do it better than I am?' Or, 'Did someone else already do it better?' 'Am I not enough?' And so in my workshops I say, bring your emotions because we're going to work with them, but not that critic, judgment, or ego. And we aim for moments of mindfulness that they can notice." Such an untangling of the actor's internal wiring may be difficult for an individual devoted to self-judgment. The concept of removing that self-doubt requires a version of microsurgery.

Some actors who have a roadblock related to self-judgment display an interesting repercussion, which in their reliance on and need to criticize others. You deflect the attention from the "sub-standard" work you feel you are doing and place it firmly on another. You find consolation by mocking or critiquing an actor, teacher, or director's work. This common pattern, like all roadblocks, has the opposite effect and draws more attention to the issue.

Another residual effect of the roadblock is defensiveness related to critique. Novello continues, "In this profession that relies on immediate feedback, the actor must accept that this process of critique is expected and necessary. How an actor processes the critique is up to them." There is a protective behavior that can occur when receiving notes or listening to peers. This is natural but can impede the work. Conversely, there are similarly overinflated egos that lack introspection and cannot hear critique. Both are safety behaviors.

## Questions to Consider

Do I enjoy the self-judgment aspect of my work?
Is my work hindered by my reliance on judgment?
Is my work helped by it?
Have I tried to leave behind any moments of judgment?
If so, what was successful?
Is there a better way for me to receive notes?
Am I judging others to avoid the work I need to do?

## Strategies

Most strategies mentioned involve retraining the communication between you and your negative thoughts. Reisberg asks actors to reorient their thoughts to dismiss any hyperbole. So, if you thought, "I was going to die of embarrassment in that scene," she suggests you, "Check your facts! No qualifiers. Or exaggeration." Similarly, you may concentrate on reframing the self-judgments and turn them into positive attributes. Similar to the inverse of your roadblock, ("— pushes on stage" to "— has high energy when performing"), you can begin to flip your thoughts of self-criticism. So while you may think, "I looked foolish up there," you may begin to alter those thoughts to, "That was pretty brave of me to get up there." It takes dedication and perseverance to reformat your thinking.

When in the studio or rehearsal hall, the inner monologue of self-judgment for the actor can be deafening. It may assist you to remind yourself to acknowledge that all others have this nagging self-judgment to varying degrees. You may learn to more healthfully accept critique by observing the culture in the room. Do others feel eviscerated by a note? Do they get defensive? If they do, what do or don't you like after observing that behavior in others? Knowing when to participate and when to observe is also important for those with a roadblock of self-judgment. If you feel that your participation when invited to offer feedback to others might help you verbalize your own issues, then participate. If you feel it may only compound your feelings of inadequacy, then you may need to remove yourself from that process.

A reminder of the importance of setting goals can also distract from the cacophony within your mind. Especially important is an honest and supportive check-in related to those goals. Goals can include a numerical rating system so your inflated language of hyperbolic doubt does not interfere with your analysis of your work. You might also look for a seamless mental activity prior to performance (like counting or spelling) to facilitate engagement in a task and distract unwanted thoughts. Third-person self-talk is also an imperative for this roadblock to remove the personal from the work. Finally, offer ways to delay judgment until after the work rather than within the performance. Having a way to chronicle a personal critique of your performance waiting just offstage or off camera may relieve you of the pressure of judgment during the work.

Moser reminds you to take care of your personal self when the professional thoughts overwhelm. He suggests, "Clear your mind. To escape self-critical internal focus, do a focus walk that is five minutes external—simply being in the moment noticing colors smells, colors—and five minutes internal. Then try it for longer periods." Your ultimate goal is to clear the mind of negative thoughts to allow a mindful approach to acting, where thoughts enter and leave without judgment.

*Supplementary Reading*

Further reading on Steven Hayes' ACT may be a great place to begin to overcome a destructive mind based on self-critique. Writings on ACT, along with the foundational writings of Henry Stack Sullivan, may be enough to vanquish the judgment roadblock. The writings of David Barlow can assist as well. These provide techniques for reappraisal of self-doubt to allow yourself the flexibility to entertain alternative possibilities.

Dr. James Gross' writings on emotion regulation, Dr. Leslie Greenberg's work on Emotion Focused Therapy to transform emotion, and Dr. Aaron T. Beck's work on cognitive reappraisal may also offer support. Reisberg suggests, "Shaun McNiff's book *Imagination in Action*. The whole book is wonderful, but particularly part three, 'To Witness Rather Than to Judge,' relates very well to what is being discussed in this section."

Hundreds of self-help books abound related to retraining negative thought. Some may resonate with your specific issues more than others. These books usually relate to the intersection of personal and professional self. The information in these books must be augmented by you to create the third level of discourse related to the character self.

## Power

There are two types of roadblocks related to power, and they are diametrically opposed. The first is an actor who is unable to assert authority in a scene. The second is an actor who is unable to relinquish power. Through these roadblocks, both types of actors have thrown the balance of the play and the character's interactions into unsupported extremes. Rarely are the best characters completely powerless or completely powerful. There are gradations of power, and the actor must be willing to explore them with that in mind.

If you are an actor who remains in the realm of the powerless, you normally play victims of the environment or society, or are under the control of other characters. This type of roadblock may appear in your work because you want the audience to sympathize or approve. Your personal relationship to power has clouded your analysis of the situation in the script. Looking over your résumé to study your past roles and their personal strength in relation to your personal definition of power may assist. Does power hold a negative connotation in your description? Marika Reisberg points out, "Gender, cultural, and familial roots may come into play with this roadblock" and the actor may have to examine past relationships with power dynamics.

Dr. Chris Hopwood explains how an actor could play the same type of dynamic throughout a multitude of characters: "It seems like it's hard for you to be cold and dominant because you are afraid that it's going to be mean or that it's going to hurt people's feelings, and they aren't going to like you; and usually you don't need to be cold and dominant. The good news is that your nice strategy works most of the time, but sometimes, you do need to be cold and dominant." So while the strategy can be rewarded, it is ultimately unsustainable.

Similarly, some actors may only play characters that dominate, have the upper hand, or control their partners. They remove any chance for intimacy, and in broader terms, they are directing the play from within their performance. By supplying strong choices and energy at the expense of craft, you have made sure that your work will be seen only as you wish it to be seen. You do not allow for other interpretations to supplant your own. This sort of actor is, as Reisberg points out, "hiding behind power."

Your roadblock with power may lie within these two extremes. Surrendering or asserting power may prove challenging, but it also leads to a fuller characterization. Power is closely linked to intimidation, and if choices are made to avoid or to rely on intimidation, they will lead you to stale or repetitive work. Intimidation also limits your choices as actor because you may feel limited to explore the opposite extreme. Having the skill to move back and forth across a broader range of power is necessary.

### Questions to Consider

Am I only making powerful or powerless choices?
What are the moments of weakness or strength that usually intimidate me in a role?
Why do I rely on power or the lack of power in my work?
Do I recognize the spectrum of choices in other actors' work that can be defined as powerful?
Do I recognize that wins and losses in a scene can expand my work?
What is the worst that can happen if I gain or lose power in a scene?

### Strategies

For many, in order to build a bridge, the focus on the roadblock through targeted scene work and improvisation related to power may prove the best strategy. Meeker actors who tend toward victimization in characterization may feel a release and gain confidence when playing characters with great power. Similarly, an actor who relies on power when acting may feel a relief when not having to drive the scene. Surrendering your prescribed and standard way of approaching a role can be liberating.

Actors who shy away from or rely on power use physical safety behaviors throughout the work to retreat from or invade the personal space of a scene partner. You may have vocal habits where you speak quietly or overpower your scene partner with volume. If these safety behaviors are pointed out, your constant use of the behaviors may lessen, and so may the roadblock.

Dr. Chris Hopwood suggests focusing on the Interpersonal Circumplex (see Figure 7.1) developed by Timothy Leary. In this unique examination of power, you may look at your character choices by seeing where the character falls on the circumplex. If your road-block is to rely on power, you may also rely on making choices that fall within the cold and dominant part of the circumplex (actors who rely on power) or you may remain safely within the warm and submissive (actors who avoid power). Through deeper reading, you may under-stand the nuances of such an approach in order to better categorize and expand your work.

Hopwood explains the need for an examination of the work you do in relation to the diagram. He suggests that an actor who relies on only the warm and submissive choices is not understanding the full range of humanity: "Sometimes people are just jerks, and you may have a hard time just being a jerk." He also recognizes the difficulty for the actor: "This is a hard pattern to break because it is so reinforced all the time.

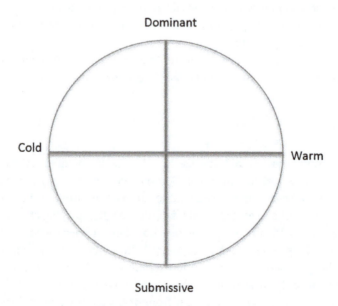

**Figure 7.1  Interpersonal Circumplex**

We all want to see the best in other people, and so that pattern is not going to be utilized very often. We all try to make people not be jerks." But he also reminds that the ability to make choices across the circle allows for a truer sense of human nature.

Hopwood provides an example of a character that can cross many areas of the spectrum with a range of experiences:

> You don't want to make a character always be cold and dominant, but there are situations like when I think of characters that get themselves into abused relationships for example. That's the person that I want to be able to distance themselves and stand up and say, "You're not doing this to me anymore. I am going to stand up for myself and do whatever I have to do to protect myself or my kids." The tricky thing is that the actor would have to be cold and submissive for the first part and eventually become warm and dominant. That is generally a hard thing to do.

Switching roles that you are working on can offer another strategy for success. By having you the play the role of your scene partner, which you have previously forced into a differential of domination or submissiveness, you can gain a clearer perspective of the other. Reisberg notes that the actor with a roadblock needs to gain "social harmony through empathy, charity, and support. It is important to build those elements." This exercise can do just that.

No matter the strategy, the actor must ultimately grant permission. You must grant permission to your scene partner to enter the scene. But you must also grant permission to yourself to allow your actor self to take power and dominate or surrender power and be the submissive follower within a scene. Those choices should be guided by the text and not by your roadblock.

### Supplementary Reading

As Hopwood noted, the writing of Timothy Leary and others on the Interpersonal Circumplex can offer a concrete entrance to fully examine a personal relationship with power. Another suggestion was reading on Vertical Dimension or Integration related to nonverbal behavior.

Reisberg suggests looking at the TED Talks of social psychologist Amy Cuddy and her exercises about body language and power. Reisberg contents, "For someone who is struggling with playing a character that is powerful, this would be a great exercise. This would also be a great exercise for self-esteem."

## Self-Esteem

Low self-esteem may be the reason you turn off the alarm and skip the audition. Low self-esteem may be the thing that makes your workout regimen inconsistent. Low self-esteem may be the reason you can't allow your work to be free.

Earlier in this book, Moser noted that every actor is "trying to fill some emotional void." This void can lead to or be based on low self-esteem. Ironically, for a business that can be seen as narcissistic and self-involved, actors notoriously have low self-esteem. Low self-esteem is related to not just your work but also your presence on stage and your willingness to risk or dare in rehearsal. It is closely related to judgment, so please be sure to read the information related to that issue as well.

Lack of confidence in your three selves can enmesh you into a tangled web of frustrations. Low self-esteem and the three selves create an even deeper self-loathing than in other people, as the professional self is on constant display. Being the focus of so many is a prime invitation for low self-esteem. Why then choose this profession when you have such an issue? The answer may be found in the third self; by becoming another person, you gain relief from a distorted self-image. When viewed through that lens, the actor with low self-esteem makes perfect sense.

While it may be more understandable, it does not eradicate the issue. Marika Reisberg reminds the actor that "self-compassion is the key. I urge the actor to seek understanding of the concept of common humanity and remind himself, 'I am not the only person who ever experienced it.'" Reisberg makes an excellent point that may offer some respite. For others, the deeply ingrained tradition of living with self-loathing will remain for a very long time.

The opposite of low self-esteem may be thought of as confidence, and for some, observing that confidence can be a very unappetizing trait. Actors who are merely confident in their craft can be thought of as cocky and make other actors with low self-esteem feel worse about themselves or jealous. Some believe that confidence in your work shows hubris. A healthy confidence in your work is to be expected. Low self-esteem often masquerades as humility.

Low self-esteem affects both introverts and extroverts. It may seem obvious (albeit misguided) that the introvert has a natural propensity to low self-esteem, as they retreat from the spotlight. The idea of an extrovert with low self-esteem may seem a bit harder to comprehend. This sort of person may cover this belief with gregarious behavior, seeking to entertain everyone while looking for way to fill the emotional void of which Moser spoke earlier.

### Questions to Consider

Do I believe low self-esteem is clouding my work as actor?
Do I find my characters all have similar low self-esteem issues?
Can I successfully portray a character that has complete confidence?
Does my low self-esteem fuel my work?
Do I enjoy the cycle of low self-esteem?
How would I describe myself as an actor?
How confident am I in my work?

### Strategies

If you suffer from low self-esteem, can you personally have a positive relationship with the actor self? Absolutely. And for some, that relationship can be a solace. Similar to the concept of losing self in performance, your low self-esteem may cause you to cling to the one thing you do best: act. The belief in your professional self can be separated from your personal self. You may be able to say. "I'm a good actor but as a person, I'm a mess."

For others though, the life of an actor can only compound your low self-esteem through constant rejection from auditions, comparison to people in the room, and seeing others similar to you achieve success. The life of an actor is competitive. And at times, the competition is overwhelming. The addition of low self-esteem to that competition only exacerbates the hard work that the actor must do.

For most, the roadblock of low self-esteem will remain throughout a career, but it can be lessened through realistic appraisals of the work performed. With lack of hyperbole, examine each performance, rehearsal, and audition in two ways. Allow your roadblock to speak first by letting out all of its reactions to the work you did that day. Once that perhaps inflated version has been shared, go back point-by-point and try to examine what actually happened with a more rational view. Another important part of that examination is asking yourself how you believe others perceived the day's work. If you can answer objectively, you may have reduced the roadblock.

Reisberg mentioned assuaging some doubts by self-compassion and acknowledging how common low self-esteem is in others as well. Perhaps use daily affirmations as a constant way to check in each day with your relationship with low self-esteem. Visualizing and projecting the view of yourself you would like to have can also assist with overcoming this roadblock. Reminding yourself after each audition, class, or rehearsal of the work that you do feel proud of as a way to a more regularized view of self can assist. Moser agrees that "finding competencies in certain areas, scaffolding, start small and building to the ultimate belief you aim for." In this case, it is a better relationship with the three selves.

Low self-esteem may be a way to spur you on to better work. If you are not satisfied with the work you are doing, continue until you are. Of course that may be very difficult based on your roadblock, but an effort on positive changes rather than negative patterns is a way to overcome this roadblock. A clearer and realistic understanding of what you hope to achieve when starting any new project can assist in better management of this issue.

## Supplementary Reading

Many of the readings from the judgment section may be useful in relation to those with the roadblock of low self-esteem. To get yourself in the growth mindset necessary for change and openness to what you have to learn, explore the writing of Carol Dweck. You may want to check out the Ted Talks and more of Dr. Brené Brown. You may also want to read *Horse Boy: A Memoir of Healing* or watch the similarly titled documentary.

## Trust

In Chapter 6, you read about an actor who lacked trust in his partners and in himself. This lack of trust is a common hurdle for most actors when life offers so many times when our trust in others evaporates. This odd profession demands that two strangers pair up at an audition and trust each other. It requires trust with a director you just met, guiding you through an especially emotional film scene. It demands trust in the ensemble that they will arrive on time to catch you when you fall as planned on an exact beat of the exact measure in the music. While the personal self may have issues with trusting the rest of the world, the actor's self demands it. And demands it freely.

What is trust? Dr. Chris Hopwood ponders:

Just think about that question. I ask many people that question. Not because I'm trying to be sneaky. "How would you define trust?" It's a hard concept. Yet everybody uses it, everybody uses it fluidly like water. "You don't trust me." "I don't trust you." "I don't trust that guy." "I've lost trust." "I don't trust anybody." It is a word that is everywhere, and when you ask people what they think it means, it takes them a long time.

Perhaps the first step to gaining trust is defining it for yourself related to your profession. What is trust to you as an actor?

Hopwood also cautions against using the word "trust" when defining the concept, as he posits, "Sometimes they can't quite grasp it. Usually they'll define it by defining the word with the word in it, 'Well I know when I trust somebody' or 'I know when I don't trust somebody because this and this happens.' So they kind get at it, but it's still not defined." Carefully address this definition, as it may hold the key for the steps and goals you set for yourself as you work through your roadblock as actor.

Moser uses a similar technique when talking to a family that lacks trust: "The concept of trust by itself is funky, and often I find [defining trust] a really nice conversation to have. It gets everyone on the same page, especially when we're talking about family, like parents and a child or a couple when there's a trust issue. That's a really great spot to start." For an actor, gaining trust means true compartmentalization. By defining and discussing trust, you may be able to offer clearer boundaries between personal and professional trust.

"In some ways, trust for an actor is like dating," says Reisberg, "You have to be willing to commit and give it a try, whatever the outcome. This may sound like having blind faith, but I think that, as an actor, there is a sense that you have to try a lot of things before you find what works for you, or choose to walk away and try something else." If you lack trust as an actor, you are always an observer outside of the world of the play, ensemble, or dramatic conflict, deciding when you may be able to commit. Reisberg suggests, "Developing the capacity to reflect on your experience would be hugely helpful. Being able to check in with yourself and see if what you tried worked for you to trust more or less. Having something to measure trust against can also be helpful. If I know what it feels like to trust myself, then I can measure other experiences against that." If you remove the element of trust from the performance equation, it reduces the basic elements of listening and responding necessary for acting. The lack of trust removes you from the stress but also from the play.

Trust is earned and develops over periods of reinforced and met expectations. Reisberg says trust is too easily expected by the actor: "We are told by our director that we need to trust ourselves or trust our scene partners regardless of whether or not that is true for us, so there is this external presence telling us how to behave, and unless we can find a way for it to come from an internal place, it will be very difficult to be authentic."

Reisberg says trust has an "internal and external focus of control. Internal means I am in charge of my life, and external means that everyone else in charge of my life. I will react or respond." Those two schools of thought can be changed, but it is easier for some than others. It may be easier "for people who grew up in community-based cultures where life was about working with others in the community. Trust is a word we throw around a lot. It goes back to value and cultural connection." Perhaps trust can be transformed from internal to external for the actor by focusing on the community-based goal of the production.

You may think that trust can be gained over time through an extended rehearsal process. That is not how this profession works. It may be the role of academic theater to provide a safe place for experimentation (and give the actor with this roadblock a chance to decide you can commit), but most projects will not offer that luxury of time. The commercial that shoots in one day, the film that has little rehearsal time, or the professional production that goes up in two weeks all demand that you overcome your issues with trust before you may be ready to do so. Get ready.

### Questions to Consider

Do I trust myself when performing?
How can I gain trust in my scene partner?
What don't I trust about the process of acting?
Have I ever felt free enough to trust when acting?
If so, what made the situation possible?
Am I and others competent enough to perform this work?

### Strategies

Trust can be linked to a "gut reaction" to a situation. Actors so often speak of the "vibe" in the audition when it may simply be a personal projection of a lack of trust. Reisberg contends, "What is that gut instinct and where is the honesty in trusting your instinct? We may have a gut feeling but won't listen to it. I'll go into sketchy part of town and flee, or I can tolerate it and stay there and be fine. So, I learn that in my gut, I was wrong. It is a deep connection." Reisberg suggests rehabilitating your connection to gut reactions based on trust. And part of gaining that trust is learning to not always trust your gut. Remember, it was your gut that allowed you to develop a roadblock with trust.

Gaining trust is also acknowledging that everyone makes mistakes and that trust cannot be shut off immediately without a chance to regain it. Reisberg says that even if an actor can begin to trust, they may lose it "because they think they see the director's machinations or that they push them too hard. How do you gain trust back? Acknowledging the humanness of everyone is one way, but how do you stick with that? How does it hold space within you?" She offers some extremely valid answers to those questions: "It's recognizing that everyone is going to make mistakes. I'm going to make a mistake—just the same as friends and family, bosses, and acting teachers. The same mistakes when you're playing the role in my mistakes." That last statement is an excellent springboard in re-examining your relationship to trust. If you can't trust others, why should they trust you? That question needs to be answered; otherwise the rehearsal hall will become a room full of actors all looking shiftily at each other, waiting for the next reason not to trust.

Actors seeking to overcome a roadblock related to trust require clarity and openness in communication. Deadlines that are met by others and requirements you must fulfill will assist in this. Perhaps setting benchmarks that if met can bring you closer to trust may work for you. Actors seeking trust also value transparency, so you may wish to ask more questions than you regularly do to offer clarity about the process. Actors with this roadblock also respond better to constructive rather than evaluative criticism, so it may be incumbent upon the actor to reframe the notes you receive into a more constructive wording for yourself.

Trust can be defensive, where you are keeping yourself safe by not letting others disappoint. Or it may be fear-based, where you worry that if you do trust, others will hurt you. In either instance, trust is earned. Trust is earned in your self and for others. Hopwood notes that, "Healing comes from acceptance that you and others are competent."

### Supplementary Reading

The first place to begin is the book, *The Body Keeps Score: Brain, Mind and Body in the Healing of Trauma* by Bessel van der Kolk. The book is an excellent source for this roadblock. Another useful concept mentioned earlier is mentalization or developing empathy for another. Looking at some of the work of A. O. Horvath and others on the Alliance Outcome Relationship to find ways to trust may prove useful. You can also look to David DeSteno's book, developed at the Northeastern University Social Emotions lab, called *The Truth about Trust: How it Determines Success in Life, Love, Learning and More.* This offers a look at trust from both a verbal and nonverbal stance. Ms. Reisberg would recommend it as a book to gain more understanding of what trust is, and how we use it in our lives. Consultants also suggested readings on post-traumatic stress syndrome and the ways in which lost trust is gained back.

## Vulnerability

"Vulnerability is," as Moser notes, "the basic roadblock! It is 'meta' and underlies everything we are talking about." Throughout this book, it has been championed as one of the main tenets of good acting and is also one of the most difficult states to achieve. Vulnerability involves a surrendering over of power to scene partners, the play, and its message. Vulnerability is the ultimate goal for this sort of work.

Vulnerability opens all bridges and is the starting point for better work that allows all other roadblocks to be addressed. It is linked to all other roadblocks, for without the ability to be vulnerable, you cannot trust, release emotion, remove judgment, or begin to address any of the other roadblocks that an actor may face. Vulnerability is complete and utter openness. Once found when acting, it is freeing and transporting.

But first, Marika Reisberg suggests, "Actors must understand why it would it be important to be vulnerable. Acting is a job of being vulnerable, that is what you are signing up for when you go to acting school, are in a show, or a film. How does it manifest itself in you personally? Vulnerability is not tangible. Some define it differently." Similar to other sections in this chapter, create a personal definition of vulnerability for you as actor. For as Reisberg notes, "Asking them to define this difficult concept forces limits. Do they think it is to be able to cry or be angry? Is it to care deeply? I'd be curious about commitment to the emotion or finding the truth." Related to the purposes of the actor, the access of emotion through the truth is what most aim for. Looking for the result (crying) reduces the attention to the commitment to the script (truth).

For some, you may believe you are being vulnerable when, in fact, you may simply be pushing the emotion or pretending to be vulnerable behind a wall. Dr. Chris Hopwood notes, "The other level is that there are things that are conscious and there are things that are unconscious, and you can have two versions of each person: one person you think you are being and one person that you are actually being." Vulnerability demands true openness in the process of finding it. Accessing a place that leaves the actor penetrable—to risk taking off the armor (or coat from an earlier analogy) you wear daily that protects you and keeps you invulnerable—is not an easy task. Being open and aware in this process is key.

Conversely, too much vulnerability is not a good thing. It can result in several outcomes. Most likely, you will be labeled "indulgent" because (as mentioned in the "A Note to Actors" introductory section) your personal catharsis took the lead over that of the character's. Self-actualized does not mean selfish. And for an actor, having access to and playing a virtuosic orchestra of emotions is seductive; that enviable access must be played in relation to the character's emotional range.

Another outcome is that you become so vulnerable that you soon lack the ability to play anything else. This issue may be quite dangerous because vulnerability bleeds over into the personal self and creates problems related to interaction in daily life. With great vulnerability comes great responsibility to keep yourself safe. Invulnerability in your personal self is a necessary component in life. It keeps you free from pain. Similarly, actors who allow the process or the teacher to push them to unsafe, vulnerable places must know when to re-armor themselves to avoid emotional distress.

I decided to include a transcript of a visit from Hopwood to class because I felt it offered unique vantage points related to vulnerability:

**Student:** So, my roadblock statement was "—substitutes true vulnerability and honesty on stage with what he deems correct or appropriate choices in acting."

**Hopwood :** So you are acting as if you were being authentic but really you are just trying to do a good job. And it's not really you, it's more of an actor version of yourself, and you would like to access your vulnerability in more than authentic way.

**Student:** Yes!

**Hopwood:** Well, part of my reaction to that is that it has got to be hard because you're an actor, so part of your job is to not be yourself, and yet you are saying that, in order to be a good actor, you have to bring yourself onto the stage and not yourself being somebody else. That is tough. My guess is that that plays out in terms of closeness to your partner. I think there are a lot of people who have a kind of false or faux closeness.

**Roznowski:** It seems from past discussions, that you have frustration and confusion with yourself because what you are trying to access is something a bit foreign or locked or untapped.

**Hopwood:** So is it that your vulnerability starts to peek through in the role and then you lose the character?

**Student:** Yes, but then I superimpose this better version of myself on at the same time or an idea of what it's supposed to be.

**Hopwood:** So it has to do with the vulnerability of "Would I be a good enough actor if I was just myself, and I don't have to put some layer on top of it?"; I do not want to get too personal, but I feel like that is what you're saying.

**Student:** Yes.

**Hopwood:** So, as an actor, how would this problem manifest itself in a relationship with another actor, and my guess is that it would manifest in terms of difficulties getting close and being real and completely open and exposed with the idea that if the other actor really knew who I really was, then they wouldn't like me. And so I have to be mostly what I am, but also with a little extra stuff. So if that were the problem, then I would try to get as close as I possibly could, with the expectation that vulnerability is going to create some anxiety. And worst-case scenario, if you are yourself and the person is going to run like hell away from you, then you just have to stay there, be vulnerable, and wait for them to come back. But if you constantly show them something honest and amazing and remarkable, then that communicates to them, even though I showed you part of me that I can't accept myself. Then, if they eventually seem to accept you so you can learn, that must not be so bad. I can be myself.

**Student:** Within the character.

**Hopwood.** Within the character. And I do not know if this personal formulation maps out to what you're saying exactly, but I think, for people who feel, "How do I be myself in the situation?" then that is how I think about it, "How can I have closeness as myself and another person on stage?"

**Another Student:** As far as, in the circumstances of the work, if it calls [for me as actor] to go to vulnerable places, whether it is feeling sad, or angry, or any combination of that, then I can pull that out for myself, but not necessarily through actually experiencing it in the scene, in the moment, from the other person.

**Hopwood:** So you can close your eyes and get yourself ready and then you can be vulnerable, but if you and I are acting together over a mutual loss or something, then that is more difficult to play in the scene? And you think, "Can I stay connected at the same time I am having a difficult emotion?" It is about being vulnerable. Going back to infancy, you need a mother's breasts, and when you get anxious that's what you need is someone to nurture you, and if you prematurely take on that role yourself, then is going to be hard to get close in the context of close feelings. You need a good scene partner who is there to receive the emotion.

In the differing questions asked by the students, we can note two very distinctive relationships with vulnerability. The first student found that just personally opening himself up was difficult on stage. His fear was that by not censoring who he really was, the scene partner, and in turn the audience, wouldn't accept him as actor. The second student found that she could find vulnerability on her own but was unable to share it with her scene partner. Both actors had an issue when it came to being open to another but in two very different ways. The trust and connection to the other can enhance vulnerability, although in these two versions the actors had not yet been able to make that discovery.

### Questions to Consider

Do I think it's possible to be vulnerable on stage?
What are the signs of vulnerability I see in other actors' performances?
Is actor vulnerability important to me?
What prevents me from being vulnerable on stage?
Why are others able to get there?
What is the worst that could happen if I am vulnerable?

### Strategies

Marika Reisberg notes, "Normalizing vulnerability can be very difficult because there are different levels of vulnerability. Some actors may be able to cry but may not be vulnerable. Others may be overly vulnerable or sensitive and that can go too far." She suggests creating a scale for vulnerability that can keep it regularized to avoid going too far, "So you can't play seven all of the time. What is the zero versus the ten? And what is the five? If you place value on it, you can begin to create a valve to access it correctly."

Moser spoke to a class related to vulnerability and a strategy to reach that elusive access for an actor:

> At the end of it all, we are all afraid of something; some of it is more complex and some of it is very simple like being afraid of dogs. Some are afraid of connectedness or intimacy and some people are afraid of vulnerability. If you write these things out and you see them through till you get to the meaning of why you fear it, then you can get to your worst fears. So this coat of armor that you want to be able to take off and be completely vulnerable in your professional life, and maybe also somewhat in your personal life, but for sure on stage. Because fear and anxieties like this are very amorphous, we start with these things that are very vague. We don't know what we really are afraid of or why we are avoiding this thing. We have some vague notion, but write out your feelings surrounding it and that can be a powerful way of opening yourself up to your own vulnerabilities on paper, and then you can finally see it from a more objective standpoint. Then you start doing your own analysis when performing [vulnerability] over time, and you start feeling, "Okay, now I get it. So it's not as scary as I thought" and then you can start taking risks and taking chances in the public arena.

Like Moser, all consultants spoke of offering outlets for practicing small moments of vulnerability—experimenting with short-term vulnerability to address a long-term roadblock. By scaffolding incrementally, the ability to access vulnerability may be more attainable. They also spoke of demonstrating personal versions of vulnerability and non-vulnerability. By understanding the two sides of the issue, you may gain better knowledge of their definitions and access points.

An interesting behavioral exercise was suggested to prove that there is a gap between higher emotion and safety behaviors. So, while safety behaviors may "keep me safe," they actually have a negative effect on my partner. You can explore your roadblock of vulnerability by using an avoidance experiment, where you avoid looking are your partner for five minutes while you talk in real life or perform your lines from a scene. Obviously the experiment will backfire because you will discover that, rather than remaining safe, you have revealed that you are obviously guarding yourself and must find more acceptable coping strategies.

Vulnerability can manifest itself in many ways, so unique strategies must be employed based on the manifestation. For the actor that masks vulnerability for perfectionism, you may be asked to work without the usual rigid support system. For the actor who cannot be vulnerable because you lack trust or empathy with your partner, you may be asked to switch roles to view things from another's perspective. For the actor too shy to be vulnerable, you may be encouraged to not censor anything anytime you speak about your work, including critique. Finding these various strategies offers focused work on the roadblock.

One of the most vulnerable things to do may be stand-up comedy. Have that student write a few jokes and tell them to the crowd. That immediate access to a vulnerable moment can be an easy entrance to deeper work. I also refer you back to the Robert Cohen exercise earlier, as well as the numerous mentions of vulnerability throughout the book.

Finding a safe and personal access to vulnerability is a primary goal for any actor. Having the resources to tap that vulnerability, as well as the wherewithal to know when to turn it off, is key. The valve that allows the actor to gauge the amount of vulnerability you use is one of the best techniques an actor can employ.

*Supplementary Reading*

Readings include the popular book, *The Marshmallow Test: Why Self-Control is the Engine of Success* by Walter Mischel. Look at the Self-Distancing writings of Ozlem Ayduk and Ethan Kross. Brené Brown's writing was again, mentioned, especially the book, *Daring Greatly: How the Courage to Be Vulnerable Transforms the Way We Live, Love, Parent and Lead*, because as Reisberg notes, "Shame and vulnerability are closely linked, and we create structures to avoid vulnerability because we are scared of shame. The book is great for looking at vulnerability." No matter the form your invulnerability takes, its power over your acting must be lessened.

# 8    Bridges

*I have never learned so much about myself as a person and as an actor before. I finally feel confident enough to recognize myself as an actor, and I think that's because I never fully understood what it meant to make big choices, how to fully submerge myself into the mind of a character, or even how to separate my emotions from a character's. I never really thought about these things before, and it really showed me who I am as a person and especially who I am as an actress. My whole life I've suffered from low self-esteem that caused me to doubt myself and criticize myself constantly, especially while I was acting. I was never confident in my acting because I felt less experienced than everyone around me, and I was always comparing myself to who I thought was a better actor than me and that did nothing but damage. I went through an emotional rollercoaster, and it was a lot to take in for me, but I learned so much about myself, such as being able to separate myself from the character, and I've accomplished getting out of my head so I can take in the moment. I am grateful to take away those things.*

In this chapter, you will complete the final steps of building a bridge to the work you seek. It also offers strategies to finally vanquish the impediments that affect your work. The final section of the chapter also offers examples of creating your personal plan for eradicating your roadblock.

In the previous two chapters you were offered numerous exercises to overcome general roadblocks and provided with strategies to address specific core issues. You have made headway in overcoming the impasse in your work. You have begun to experiment and test the tenacity of your current roadblock in acting. You understand its effect on your work and have begun the process of releasing its hold. What remains is a way to build a permanent bridge to the type of work that you want to do in the future: work that remains open and bold; choices that extend beyond your safe and standard few; confidence that is renewed and fearless. The bridge you are hoping to construct requires clear goals and strategic planning, a bridge that will propel you to transcend your roadblock.

## How Can I Get Out of My Own Way?

Actors often overcome their roadblocks with the simple phrase "I got out of my own way." In its basic essence that means giving yourself permission to do the work you know you should do. For actors, getting out of your own way means diving in and playing the scene with full commitment. For some actors, the heightened frustration of dealing with the identified roadblock allows you to finally and fully shed your inhibitions, to daringly jump in, and achieve peak performance. The risk you take is born from annoyance at the limitations in your work. Tired of self-examination or fed up with the lack of freedom related to your craft, you summon up the energy and fortitude to play the scene fully and eradicate the roadblock. You got out of your own way. You gave yourself permission.

More often than not, you surprise yourself or lose yourself by diving into the work so boldly. The catharsis you feel is triply satisfying because it fulfills all three selves. The personal self is satisfied that private issues have not affected the work; the professional self is thrilled to have a new range of choices; and the character self is excited to have been played honestly and fully. You have achieved peak performance. There is no greater thrill for an actor. Those moments when you get out of your own way are joyful causes for celebration that set a new standard for the way you will perform in the future. Certainly habits and safety behaviors may creep back into your work, but usually, the experience of bridging a roadblock (again, excuse the mixed metaphors) becomes a benchmark for future acting.

While that moment of success is common in this sort of work, others may take tentative steps toward their freedom in acting. This is because you may feel paralyzed by such intense concentration on one aspect of your work. Most commonly you may say, "I was in my head" or "I was watching myself." Both complaints reveal that you are working toward overcoming the roadblock, but perhaps you are working too hard. The section on intellectualizing in Chapter 6 provided some strategies, but if those do not work, there are others that you can explore here. The strategies are repetition, focus on the other, and goals.

### Repetition

Like any new skill, in order to perfect it, you must practice, rehearse, and repeat it until you have understood its complexities, and most likely, at some point in the process you will fail. That failure can prevent you from trusting that you can eventually become a master craftsmen, but the reality is that most actors have the capacity to find freedom in your work; you just do not have access currently to the correctly routed pathways. Like any skill, it requires repetition.

Dr. Jason Moser notes, "It's like, 'Let's work out in the gym, so that when I come to a situation in my life and this large boulder comes rolling down and its going to fall on me, I'm ready to catch it because I've been working out so much.' By doing this day in and day out, you're going to be ready, even if say you're not there yet. But you will know what do eventually." This idea of exercise and repetition allows the actor to gain the strength and skills to master a usually untapped emotional life. Moser continues, "You're working this brain muscle out that deals with emotional flexibility, and that's what you want to promote. You want to promote emotional and cognitive flexibility because you need to be in and out of different states of emotion and cognition and then back again." The apt metaphor of the gym is something that may be able to remove the onus of immediate perfection and can create a regimented approach to your ultimate goal.

Dr. Chris Hopwood approaches the same philosophy from a more clinical stance that espouses the need for repetition: "I would imagine you have to keep going back to the same thing, and challenging yourself over and over. This is consistent with Learning Theory. You don't teach a mouse how to get to the cheese through a maze with one trial; you have to keep teaching it over and over, and that's how memory works in the brain." The need for repetition is physiological. Hopwood continues, "Our assumption is that you usually learn roadblocks for a good reason. It's not like just pointing them out to somebody is going to automatically change him or her. I would imagine it takes a lot of playing different characters with a lot of the same kinds of issues in order to challenge the roadblock over and over again." It takes exercise.

The need for repetition is clear. The more you can exercise with a healthy degree of focus on the actual process rather than the result, the more likely it is that you will become agile enough to build the bridge to the work you desire. The idea of repetition and exercise can be put into action through the scene work or strategies already discussed such as targeted journaling, meditation, and the setting of clear goals. Finding the right exercise can prepare you for peak performance.

**Exercise 8.1** Daily exercise. Set aside a few minutes each day and redo the provided exercises, read on related issues, or create your own exercises that will target your specific roadblock

### Focus on the other

You understand the benefits of addressing roadblocks: you will become a more adept, more vulnerable, and more skilled actor. That understanding may be impeded by a fixation on creating the bridge to your peak work. Redirect that focus where it needs to ultimately be: on your scene partner. Just because you are working on a specific aspect of your professional self, you must not forget the basics of acting that include listening and responding to another. It is hard to be in the moment when your current focus is internal. By placing your focus on, and more importantly trust in, your partner, you can most easily build the bridge to less self-conscious acting.

Some students reported that they were frustrated that they were able to get to vulnerable places through the help of a scene partner but lacked the ability to do this on their own. The use of the partner is to be encouraged as it shows a basic understanding of working in tandem while listening and responding. The reliance on the other in creating a bridge is integral. So, rather than diminish that achievement, you must recognize professional success. While the actor may be unable to get there personally, your success in achieving vulnerability with a partner shows a successful lack of negative internal focus. It places your focus on your intended target: your scene partner.

Cultivating external focus is important for the actor. As mentioned, it should be aimed at the scene partner, but if necessary, the actor can also begin to use other externals to keep their outward attention, such as an object within your sight line, an exact spot in the room, or a specific area of your partner's face. This shift of focus from internalized distraction to external stimuli is key. As Moser notes, "Because fortunately, and unfortunately, the internal world can be the best place and the worst place because its where we get our reflection and ideas, but it's also the place that sucks us in, and we mess up so many things in the external world that way."

The outward focus when performing is a necessity, while retaining an inward focus is essential for pre- and post-performance assessment. The freedom you usually find in peak performance (when nothing else is remembered other than an almost out-of-body experience) does not rely on any internal focus other than the inner monologue of the character. Ultimately, there is the alchemy of two actors plying their craft, each to their fullest abilities. Moser notes, "As much as you can be out in the world, as much as you can be listening and reacting to what's happening in the moment, the better off you will be." This is the essence of good acting, and its reintroduction in this chapter is a reminder of that.

## Exercise 8.2   Outward focus. Perform the scene focusing only on the other

### Goals

Building the bridge to your best professional self requires the setting of goals. It requires you to create a foundation and then build up, step by step and layer by layer, to create a solid support system for the work you want to do. It requires the understanding of incremental growth and an ability to see how one step leads to the next. Since every actor's bridge requires unique materials, most of this work is carried out alone.

Creating a hierarchical strategy to reach your ultimate goal is key, and only you can determine which roles, exercises, or characters cause you more incremental anxiety. In order to "get out of your own way," you may need to examine the levels of fear this work causes in you. The character actor may find that approaching roles too similar to yourself is paralyzing, while the personality actor most fears the roles that require drastic transformation. The goals for each are to begin to find tactics that inch you closer and closer to the work you most fear. By setting these goals, you may soon find that you have clearly defined what success means to you. Once you have achieved your goal, try tackling a role that is slightly more difficult until the roadblock is overcome. You may even choose to use the same scene but set goals for the next run according to how deeply you will incorporate the work that scares you. Such practical goal-setting can offer a productive way to incrementally build a bridge.

It is sometimes easier to "diagnose" and "treat" another than it is for you to do this yourself. This next exercise offers another way of setting goals by using a character you have performed, are studying, or have always wanted to play. Examine the roadblocks that affect that character. The roadblocks for the character most likely extend to a "personal" issue. Use your analytical skills (both script- and roadblock-based) and start to diagnose these fictional characters and decide for them the work they must do in order to bridge them to a fuller "life." While you may already undertaken a version of this in character analysis, this new focus on the roadblock may reveal new ways to analyze a character. This exercise can possibly show you where you need to do more research or examination and help you to prioritize goals.

Characters from recognizable plays and films are great places to start. Using some categories from the book (see the sections on "Anxiety," "Intimacy," "Body Awareness," and so on in Chapter 7), you can begin to examine the roadblocks you see affecting iconic roles. Hamlet's lack of trust related to his father's murder. Blanche DuBois' fear of appearing unattractive to others. Mama Rose's need for power in all she does. You will write about your diagnosis of their roadblocks and create a plan to a more satisfying "life" for these great characters. Once you understand the basic roadblock, you can next examine the unique emotional situations that playing them would require. The flexibility an actor needs to play such iconic characters should become clear. What roadblocks must be overcome in order to truly inhabit the role? For example, how can an actress with a roadblock related to a fear of portraying high emotional stakes successfully play the histrionic character of Alma Winemiller in *Summer and Smoke?*

## Exercise 8.3  Diagnose a character. Using the knowledge you have gained about roadblocks, examine a fictional character

It may be interesting for you to find characters with your personal roadblock. Try that role on for a bit through scene or monologue work. What does that similarity feel like? How does it feel to find someone with the matching of roadblocks? Is it freeing or is it even more constricting? When looking at this roadblock, does the removal of self make you more empathetic to this character's similar struggle?

Moser reminds us of the hard work we are doing:

> A lot of this has to do with commitment to making a change, and your commitment and focus that you're doing this on purpose. So much has to do with control. "I'm committing to changing it so now it's under my control. It's not controlling me." As soon as you make that mindset change that, "Now I'm going to do something about it," then when it comes time to do these things in a show, in a class, you've prepared yourself and you're now in control of it.

By setting strategic goals and targeting the ways in which you can get there, you can control you fears, quieten the negative thinking, and build the bridge to the work you want to do. Moser concludes, "As a little caveat to anything I'm saying: I realize it is very difficult. It takes commitment, it takes time and energy, and none of it is easy."

## Why Can't I Get There All of the Time?

Hopefully you have achieved some moments of victory related to your roadblock, but the question remains, "How can I take these little nuggets of success and expand on them?" An exploration of how you arrived at such a moment is key, but what drew you out of those moments is also important. It can reveal triggers that allow and deny access to the work you want to be doing.

Those moments of successfully stifling your roadblock are revelatory. Hopwood notes, "Yes, it's the 'aha' or the insight of 'I just learned something about myself,' or 'I just pulled myself out of this pattern.' Those are the rare and precious moments when you feel like you're doing something useful." The elation you feel, however brief, can spur you on to taking bolder and deeper risks in your work. Celebrate that moment and make that your new level of expectation within your acting work, rather than allowing yourself to expect your previous way of working.

You may feel frustration about this momentary success within a scene and become angered at losing the connection. Hopwood offers another way of looking at this issue of sporadic success: "The rare moments and positive behavior should be reinforced, and you don't want to punish the bad behavior." So, allow yourself to revel in those moments of good acting. These prove that you are capable of the work you wish to achieve. You have begun to build the bridge.

As educator, you may find yourself confused as to the best way to coach these moments of intermittent success. Following the student's lead, you can ask probing questions related to the ways in which the student accessed the place they felt was a success and try to assist them in identifying what drew them out of the work they achieved. Help the student to construct ways to analyze patterns in their work. In your role as educator, you want to mentalize with your students. Mentalization is a way to empathize and understand the state of another. By empathizing with the student and understanding the possible confusion and frustration related to this erratic performance, you can more easily offer coaching that is healthful and helpful. While this is an approach you may do daily, the difficult process of building the bridge to better acting may mean that this strategy bears repeating.

To assist the actor in creating consistent access to their imagined work, carefully chosen scene work is necessary. Moser notes, "Choose roles that are purposefully out of their control zone to broaden their horizons." For the student who has an issue with avoiding vulnerability through comedy, a natural choice would be a scene that had high dramatic stakes and demands a respect and attention to risk and dramatic conflict. Similarly, wisely chosen scenes can create a culture of danger and experimentation in the studio. Again, while you may already choose scene work that pushes the actor to new choices, now, newly armed with their guidance, you can assist them in finding work specifically targeted to the issues they have self-identified.

## Exercise 8.4   Targeted scene work

Another pattern that occurs linked to sporadic success is the return to safe and standard choices. You may feel that the connection you made in the scene proved you have vanquished your roadblock, but that muscle needs constant exercise, and your habitual standard and safe place that you once acted from still remain the most accessible. In order to make the bridge permanent, your approach to analyzing a character demands an expansion of your past process to include the possibilities within the new areas you have mastered. In order to maintain their potency, the new skills you have acquired must be used regularly. So, when approaching an audition, a new role, or a scene, ask yourself if you are also analyzing with the addition of your new skill set, or has that dastardly roadblock resurfaced and compelled you back to the work on the other side of the bridge?

To keep those skills fresh, I suggest regular targeted improv that allows you to exercise the skills you have previously mastered. Find a character, situation, and environment that will push you the furthest toward accessing your bridged professional self. Allow that scene to test your limits to make sure that this new area of your work remains open and accessible.

## Exercise 8.5   With another, improvise a scene that specifically targets the roadblock

While this may be in opposition to references earlier as to the best ways in which introverts work, you can easily adapt this, or any exercise in the book, for introverts or extroverts. In this exercise, you can offer several adjustments:

allow the improvise to improvise a scene using characters that they are familiar with and know well; or, allow them to run a scene that they have rehearsed in which they have succeeded at overcoming their roadblock and can focus solely on new choices. If adopting the latter, make sure to set attainable new goals for the scene. Augment the focus of the exercises based on the individual. Adjusting earlier exercises for an extrovert may mean that targeted journaling is replaced by group discussion. Such a revision for all exercises can occur.

As you begin to more clearly understand the parameters of your roadblock, do not be surprised when the roadblock begins to morph. This is another common aspect of the work. Once you have (to use Marika Reisberg's Chapter 4 analogy) peeled away some layers of the onion, you may see that what you thought was the issue is actually something else. Students have noted that, "I find that my roadblock is morphing. It changes, and through one discovery about the roadblock—it is getting redefined, so you think, 'okay that's somehow connected, maybe not linearly, but somehow this leads to that.'" Another questioned, "But do you feel that we are trying to get to the nugget, the core, or that it's just a barrage of all interconnected goals?" Another offered, "I think it's all unique, from person to person because, personally, I feel like I started out giving my roadblock statement as, not necessarily generic, but surface level, but after tackling that scene, I was able to say 'okay, this is really where I am' and I was able to get a more solidified roadblock statement as opposed to the initial statement I had." This transformation is quite natural and should not cause alarm.

The phenomenon of the morphing roadblock has many possibilities. The most likely is that, through a deeper examination of the three selves, you have found that your first roadblock statement offered a more superficial view of deeper issues. You may also have been misled through initial assessments that the data pointed to one area but through more personal reflection, you have found a related or unrelated issue. You may also find the roadblock is connected to two or three issues, depending on the acting work you are doing, and so a different barrier appears. The morphing of the roadblock usually requires a repetition of some of the past work in order to understand its new focus.

Part of creating a bridge to the work you want is gaining more autonomy in your craft. The reliance on outside critique may start to be replaced by deeper self-reflection and taking responsibility for the type of work you want to create. This required reflection looks at the roadblock holistically and constantly. Such reflection does not end in the classroom or in performance.

More than likely, an actor who is serious about addressing roadblocks may begin to see those professional behaviors occur in personal interactions. So the actor who uses humor to avoid intimacy may find that, in his real life, he does this as well. It is natural to notate such personal moments when unwanted professional patterns occur. The actor who wants to play something other than comedic roles may choose to address that in his personal life but certainly does not have to. His goal is access to those emotions while performing. So he may choose to keep others at a distance and laughing in real life, while he concentrates on accessing the dramatic work he desires in the rehearsal room. Identifying roadblocks and safety behaviors from various personal vantage points, rather than only from a professional point, may offer deeper clarity of your understanding of the barrier. The awareness of those real-life safety behaviors and their uses (whether addressed personally or not) can certainly hasten the bridge's construction. The residual effect is a continual reliance on self-awareness and self-critique rather than seeking outside verification of your roadblock. When creating a bridge statement, this removal of reliance on others for feedback in favor of a clearer process for self-examination can become a key component.

## What Is a Bridge Statement?

In conjunction with your original, or now updated, roadblock statement, this new declaration is a contract of sorts to create the plan for bridging your work to the place you imagine it can be. This statement offers realistic and clear instructions on how to create the bridge based on your intimate knowledge of all aspects of the roadblock. All of the self-reflection, exercises, struggles, and successes now lead to a plan that will create the work you are capable of and that you desire.

A bridge statement can be quite simple and offer practical strategies for future acting work. Writing in the third person creates a simple proposition similar to this: "—'s roadblock is that he uses humor to avoid vulnerability on stage, and in order to bridge that, he will invest in the dramatic given circumstances of the script, match the tone and energy of his partner, and risk going to emotional territory."

The bridge statement requires a distillation of the roadblock and its solution. You will note it does not bring in the work that your personal self may do—the bridge statement is for you as actor. So while the personal self may recognize that humor is merely a defense mechanism to avoid emotional honesty in real life, the bridge statement addresses the professional self.

## Exercise 8.6 Write a bridge statement

Below are a few examples of bridge statements created by students in classes devoted to roadblocks:

> *— makes small physical choices to avoid making the wrong ones, and in order to bridge that, she will create characters with different body centers and gesture ranges and experiment with working "outside in."*
>
> *— controls his partner in order to make sure the scene goes as he has planned, and in order to bridge that, he will relinquish power in rehearsal and performance and allow his partner to drive the process.*
>
> *— is so hyper-critical of her work that she is constantly directing herself, and in order to bridge that, she will invest in staying in the moment by not setting any blocking and reducing her inner monologue to one simple phrase.*
>
> *— needs to be liked by the audience and demands their approval, and in order to bridge that, she will spend more time finding darker motivations in script analysis and create a list of more selfish objectives to use in upcoming scenes.*
>
> *— finds safety in playing the victim, and in order to bridge that, he will make more aggressive choices that include intimidation, control, and destruction of the other.*
>
> *— relies on his ability to play many outlandish characters on stage, having never once been honest, and in order to bridge that, she will simplify her process and begin with her personal similarities to the character rather than differences.*

The bridge statement can be refined similarly to your revision of the roadblocks statement, as you try various strategies to finally wrest power from the barrier that has been holding you back. Creating that practical bridge statement is one of the final steps to finding freedom in your work. The bridge statement is also a clear way to offer the educator a rubric for coaching. Did the student fulfill the goals set out in the scene work? As an example, your feedback for an actor trying to overcome her issue of speeding though her work in order to avoid honesty could be focused on, "Was the actor able to achieve the stillness in the scene that she suggested?" These bridge statements offer an entrance and invitation to the healthful coaching that keeps both educator and actor on proper ground.

The journey to this moment required patience and acute self-awareness. It began with grasping the concept of roadblocks, examining your professional work, the assessments, and the introduction of the three selves. From there, you began to formulate your roadblock statement, understand its hold in all of its forms in your acting work, attack it with vigorous exercise, and finally craft this clear and concise contract to create an entrance to the work you know you are capable of. You have given yourself power over this area of limitation in your past work.

The bridge statement is a solution-based approach to the level of work you wish to perform regularly. For some, the bridge statement is all you need. You understand what you need to do and you do it—instant success. For some, the use of this contract may not immediately break through the roadblock, but it should offer a means by which you can lessen its power in your acting. Still for others, you may find that going back and repeating some of the exercises provided in this book, or creating some of your own specifically related to your issues, will reduce the roadblock until it merely becomes a distraction rather than a focus. Some may find that, armed with your strategy, you can begin to make targeted, smaller, yet safer, assaults on the roadblock, and by chipping away at its armor, you have lessened its power. You might make peace with your roadblock and acknowledge its presence in your craft, but will not let it define your work. No matter the result, the deep reflection on your process throughout the roadblock investigation has allowed you to take ownership of your work, have a sharper understanding of your personal approach, and have a healthier delineation of selves. In many ways, through a deeper understanding of your relationship to acting, the bridge has already been built.

The lack of freedom, the self-consciousness, the fear, the anxieties, and all those negative thoughts and feelings that impacted your past work can be released by crossing the bridge to unencumbered work. The roadblock that impeded your path and corralled your choices into one safe zone can now be removed to allow you to explore your craft in new ways. Your process can now take on a sense of mindfulness.

# 9    Mindfulness

*The freedom in making what seemed like scary choices that I had found the*
*ability to make in class was something that I tried to remind myself of in*
*every rehearsal. I reached a point where I wasn't watching myself from the*
*audience's perspective as I had done so often in the past, and I was living*
*as the character with total mindfulness of that character's thoughts and*
*objectives. This was a way for me to take the lessons I had learned in a*
*classroom setting and apply them to a real and complete project.*

This book began with a thorough examination of your craft as actor
through self-analysis, data collection, and diagnostic testing. In the previous chapters, you were offered ways to overcome, circumvent, or eradicate your identified roadblock. You have created a bridge to the work
you wish to do. Your work may now take on a sense of mindfulness.

The goal during performance is mindfulness. Mindfulness for the
actor includes several planes of existence: as your personal self, who
understands the extreme situations in which you are placing yourself
are pretend and temporary; as your professional self, who works to
maintain healthy and positive working habits; and as the character self,
where the only roadblocks are those presented by the writer. Dr. Jason
Moser notes, "To achieve mindfulness, one must find complete openness to the experience."

For actors, that implies an understanding of the stressful situations
(performing) in which you put yourself. It also means an acceptance
that the pressure related to performance can be lessened by the recognition and acceptance of this three-layered plane on which an actor
must harmoniously exist. Mindfulness allows you to accept the stress of
exposing your emotions in front of others and invites you to maintain
a nonjudgmental awareness of this distinctive profession. The concept
of mindfulness is a popular philosophy for many; for an actor, it has a
uniquely expanded quality that also includes a fictional self.

Mindfulness has its roots in Buddhism, and was later adopted and
adapted by Jon Kabat-Zinn. Evidence of its transformative powers in
both personal and professional lives is ubiquitous. There are readings,

videos, and coaches readily available to assist with mindfulness for both personal and professional selves. What concerns us is how these concepts and precepts are adapted for the actor.

The thirteenth-century Persian poet Mewlana Jalaluddin Rumi wrote a poem entitled, "The Guest House," and this holds extraordinary prescience for your purposes. In the poem, every person is a dwelling where each day a new emotion (or guest) may visit, and, whether they are good or bad emotions, they bring us closer to self-awareness. As an actor, the metaphor takes on a double meaning.

### The Guest House
**translated by Coleman Barks**

This being human is a guest house.
Every morning a new arrival.

A joy, a depression, a meanness,
some momentary awareness comes
As an unexpected visitor.

Welcome and entertain them all!
Even if they're a crowd of sorrows,
who violently sweep your house
empty of its furniture,
still treat each guest honorably.
He may be clearing you out
for some new delight.

The dark thought, the shame, the malice,
meet them at the door laughing,
and invite them in.

Be grateful for whoever comes,
because each has been sent
as a guide from beyond.

This concept has been adapted into an exercise used quite often in mindfulness work called "The Uninvited Guest," where different guests (in this case emotions) arrive at your house, and who you more than likely do not want to deal with. The concept of the exercise is to invite these negative emotions in. Sit with them for a bit. "Converse" with them. Understand them. And although the uninvited guests may be unpleasant company for an actor, a full-scale understanding of a broad spectrum of emotions and feelings is necessary. Of course this and all the other exercises presented in this book can be readily found in substantially more detail online, in articles and videos, in books, and through coaches.

Yet another mindfulness exercise can be adapted specifically for the actor to better understand a sense of the three selves: the mountain meditation. In this exercise, you think of yourself as a mountain, an immovable and unchangeable part of the landscape. Life's weather (worries) happen around you while you remain fixed. In adapting the exercise for the actor, perhaps think of the three selves. Your personal self is the mountain, and despite the highly emotional territory you must "experience," you will remain that constant. Spinning wildly round you are your two other two selves who live in a higher emotional state. The professional self and character self can be thought of as the weather, the wind, and the seasons, all fleetingly swirling around the mountain, which remains unfazed by their haphazardness. For the actor, the volatility of the emotional availability of the professional and character selves calls for a strong connection to a resilient personal self. Mindfulness can be extremely helpful for keeping the actor's personal health at the fore.

Meditation (see also Exercise 6.23) is a powerful tool in relation to successfully eradicating the roadblock. Through meditation you can set goals, prepare for performance, or cool down after an exceptionally exhausting emotional performance. Meditation takes various forms beyond the lotus-positioned image most commonly pictured. For an actor, it could mean a post-show shower, quiet time in a dressing room, or a ride home on the subway without the distraction of music or reading. It is a chance to envision or reflect on a performance or an audition. Rather than the targeted and focused meditation described in Chapter 6, in mindfulness, the openness to the experience allows thoughts to flow freely and drift, without guidance or judgment.

This same openness is what is sought when performing on stage—an actor who is available to the needs and choices of a scene partner. Similarly, you are available to your emotions—an actor focused on the scene but with nonjudgmental observation, who acknowledges the worries of lost lines, unresponsive audiences, and overcoming your road-block, but with evaluative rather than judgmental thought. Essentially, you are retraining yourself to think about what works and what needs revision rather than what went horribly and what you ruined. You are developing your "observer self" as an actor. The observer self is one who can be in the moment, compassionately aware of the situation, yet unaffected by stress.

By relieving the pressure of self-judgment, mindfulness offers a less disturbing access to the rich emotional life necessary for the actor. Those difficult moments of vulnerability, honesty, and intimacy are made readily available through mindfulness. Moser sees the benefits: "I think these meditations on emotions can help you gain greater awareness in the moment of how your emotions fluctuate, how your thoughts fluctuate." He describes the activity as sitting with your eyes closed, observing the experience, and questioning what is happening as you focus on an emotional goal. As you think about accessing vul-nerability, allow yourself the time to explore all aspects of that emo-tion and its connection to you and your experiences with it—pleasant or unpleasant. Allow your thoughts to flow uninterrupted to your full understanding of vulnerability. The same nonjudgmental attitude is necessary for all mindfulness practices. It is then that you may more fully understand your relationship with an area that has been blocked.

Mindfulness is a state of being many actors (and humans in general) desire, but as Moser points out, "Mindfulness is a skill that requires prac-tice like anything else. It requires time, effort, and commitment, just like exercising. Those seem to be prerequisites for developing any skill with any effectiveness." This focus is also necessary in an augmented studio setting. Moser continues, "The actor and teacher have to dedicate time to both sit for meditation to gain mindfulness skills as well as apply other concepts like the 'present-moment focus' or 'walking mindfulness meditation.' The actor must cultivate this so as to take advantage of this skill building and ultimately become the way of being." While this is the desired goal for open acting, the chance for such reflection must be allowed throughout the process through devoted class or rehearsal time as well as personal time.

The two concepts mentioned in the previous quote can be (and are) easily used in acting classrooms. The "walking mindfulness meditation" is an ambulatory meditation that asks the participant to walk with-out purpose. Rather than your usual destination-oriented movement, this nonlinear walk allows the thoughts to enter and leave the brain without a prescribed path or boundaries. "Present-moment focus" is becoming aware of the things around you in various circles of attention (in the studio) or in relation to you (your clothing, the temperature). Sometimes even labeling or naming the things in the room—"the red chair"; "the broken clock"; "my blue skirt"—can be a way for students who have carried out highly emotional work to return to the present. Other cool-down methods so highly advocated for in Maxwell, Seton, and Szabó's, "The Australian Actors' Wellbeing Study" may include repetitive hobbies such as knitting; the mindless watching of kitten videos; mindful walks to take in the surroundings; gaming that is non-violent and less head-centered; other human interaction (not about the show); or nearly anything that distracts from the past, emotionally charged work of the professional and character self and returns you peacefully to the present. Mindful cool-down methods eschew the usual post-show drinking actors so often do to distract or decompress from a performance, and pave the way for healthier alternatives. Just as importantly, mindfulness can help an actor to leave the drama behind her following performances by doing mindfulness exercises that purposefully negate emotions—by "uninviting" these same emotions summoned for the performance. Once again, the unique world of acting needs unique strategies.

It is also important to have a healthy and active personal life. Actors consumed with their craft often forget this strategy. Dr. Mark Seton, one of the main architects on the Australian study, has investigated the wellbeing of actors in the workplace and in training in the UK and in Australia. Dr. Seton believes that

> the healthiest actors are those who can value and invest in their everyday lives alongside any commitment they may have to acting as a profession. It is these actors' capacity to remain open, vulnerable, and connected through genuine human interactions that enables them to be available to "touch and be touched" by the text and by their fellow actors when they work on an acting job.

He advocates that time away from the professional self can lead to a more mindful and healthy actor.

For the educator, mindfulness can be just as important for growth in the classroom. Having an educator who embraces and practices mindfulness can create the "safe environment" espoused by so many. It is surprising how many mindfulness concepts can be easily adapted for standard acting exercises. Some main precepts of mindfulness can be found on nearly any acting syllabus. They include, "focus on what's right in front of you"; "focus on your breathing"; "focus on your inner body"; "feel the energy of others present"; and "surrender to the emotion that is already there." These main precepts of mindfulness correlate strongly to the studio exercises involving observation, imagination, relaxation, and the fundamental value of listening and responding. Adapting these or other concepts to create a studio that allows for the self-reflection necessary to create more facile artists is key.

Another benefit to mindfulness is the actor's gained independence from the reliance on a director or teacher's feedback. Retaining a sense of freedom within your choices, and armed with an open mind that allows for reflection rather than judgment, you may actually gain autonomy in a profession normally guided by the critique of others. By becoming a more self-actualized actor, you may be able to accept and guide your work through a better sense of self and your craft.

I asked Dr. Chris Hopwood about the specific struggles for an actor related to the concept of mindfulness. I asked, "How can an actor achieve mindfulness when they spend so much time in their head?" He replied, "Not just actors, but I think we all struggle with this in our culture. As you know, there are a lot of techniques, like yoga, meditation, and athletics that should help people get out of their heads. It is possible that deeper reading about Buddhism or mindfulness could be a good use of students' time."

Mindfulness is not for everyone and the time spent with your eyes shut meditating, imagining yourself as a mountain, inviting emotions into your home, or any of the concepts covered may make some actors feel uncomfortable, roll their eyes, or completely shut down. Even though, as actors, we spend our lives working in imaginary worlds, this sort of metaphorical immersion may be something you do not respond to. For this reason, I did not include exercises in this chapter, since you can seek them on your own, should the concepts interest you. You need not accept a full conversion to mindfulness in order to be a good actor; however, I do think that the basic concepts may offer any actor relief from negative self-doubt or constant judgment that have limited so many. On a basic level, mindfulness allows for emotional accessibility with an incisive self-awareness of the three selves for an actor.

You may respond more easily to less metaphorical practices, such as improvisation. Placing yourself in the constant state of invention that improvisation provides can create a freedom in your acting (like the actor discussed in Chapter 1) and extinguish self-consciousness. In order to keep such continual self-reflection at bay, you may embrace some of the concepts contained in the book only for immediate pre-performance work. You may use the bridge statement as a mantra for performance. Whatever your mode of learning or your adaptation of the concepts within the book, your aim should be to sustain the bridge to better work that you have created and maintain its structure.

If you are still struggling with a roadblock, remind yourself that the strategies of the bridge statement may be revised as you continue to work on your roadblock. Retaining an open, mindful attitude is the answer. Should you still need assistance, you may return to the exercises presented throughout the book or create some on your own. You may also augment your self-defined strategies with reading from Chapter 7. A continuing assessment, in conjunction with realistic goals related to your roadblock, is necessary. Its power will lessen. It is then up to you to cultivate your newly unfettered work. Through your individual attention to your craft, you will create a personal system and strategies to consistently deliver the performance you imagine.

## What Lies Beyond the Bridge?

By reading to this point, either as educator or as actor, you understand the process of eliminating roadblocks. The bridge statement, in conjunction with mindfulness in performance, is the goal for the actor. The combination of these two elements can assist you in finding the openness that you lacked when you started this journey.

What lies beyond the bridge is unencumbered acting—acting without the self-imposed limits that have corralled your work into safe and careful areas—and, most importantly, greater access to the elusive peak performance.

You have most likely achieved a bridge to the work you want to do, and the choices available to you are expansive. This is the first step to achieving the peak performance for the actor through a combination of freedom, unlimited choices, and mindfulness that intersects all three selves and allows those rare moments on stage when an actor is transported beyond any limitations: acting without roadblocks.

Dr. Thalia R. Goldstein, an expert on acting and psychology, reveals what she believes every actor needs:

> I've written a lot about the skills that I think undergird acting. I think the big three are: 1) Theory of mind (the ability to understand what a person is thinking, or feeling); 2) Empathy (the ability to feel emotions of a character, to take their emotional perspective); and 3) Emotion regulation (the ability to understand and change emotions in oneself in order to best portray the emotions of a character on stage). Add to those three cognitive and emotional skills, the physical nature of being able to portray an emotional state and intention in such a way that an audience can read what you are doing, and an understanding generally of how emotions, personality states, skills, knowledge and traits work, and you've got an actor!

Those qualities are what this book has been about, especially how they work between and within the three selves:

1. Theory of mind—You have a deeper understanding of your personal cognition, your professional self's motivation, and their connection to the creation of a character's mind.

2. Empathy—You have gained a deeper empathic understanding of how your personal issues may impact your work. You have sympathized with your professional self for the hard work an actor must do daily. And you have assumed the thoughts without judgment of a variety of characters.

3. Emotional regulation—This most difficult aspect of acting is where most roadblocks have been hiding across all three selves. It is through the destruction of the emotional regulation barrier that you may find freedom in performance.

When fully embodied, Dr. Goldstein reminds us, "You've got an actor!"

Throughout the book, you have explored your work in great detail and know it intimately. You are in charge of the choices you make on stage and off, based on your awareness of the three selves. The diagnostic tests and exercises allow you a new way of looking at your work. You have examined your process through various assessments and exercises and examined your roadblock from numerous vantage points, lessening its tight grip on your work. Practical exercises allow you to explore your work in untapped ways. You have made a contract for the work that you wish to do in the future. And you can now ply your craft with an ability to let the clouded mind of performance in the past remain open and free of unwanted distractions when performing.

With this newfound freedom, unlimited access to new choices, and a properly directed internal/external focus, you may achieve peak performance.

As you continue to master your craft, another area of limitation may reveal itself in the future. That is to be expected. Rather than dreading it, enjoy the process of expanding your toolkit, reinvigorating your craft, and continuing the journey of self-discovery. Being an adept, skillful, and vulnerable actor means a life-long quest to perfect your work.

# Bibliography

Ayduk, Ozlem, and Ethan Kross. "Pronouns Matter When Psyching Yourself Up." *Harvard Business Review*, February 6, 2015. Web. Date accessed: August 25, 2016. Available at: https://hbr.org/2015/02/pronouns-matter-when-psyching-yourself-up.

Barlow, David H., and Michelle G. Craske. *Mastery of Your Anxiety and Panic*. Oxford: Oxford University Press, 2007.

Beck, Aaron T. *Cognitive Therapy and the Emotional Disorders*. New York: International Universities, 1976.

Benjamin, Lorna Smith. *Interpersonal Diagnosis and Treatment of Personality Disorders*. New York: Guilford, 1996.

Blair, Rhonda. *The Actor, Image, and Action: Acting and Cognitive Neuroscience*. London: Routledge, 2008.

Bornstein, Robert F. "A Process Dissociation Approach to Objective-Projective Test Score Interrelationships." *Journal of Personality Assessment*, vol. 78 no. 1 (2002), 47–68. Web. Date accessed: February 20, 2016. Available at: http://www.tandfonline.com/doi/abs/10.1207/S15327752JPA7801_04?src=recsys&.

Brown, Brené. *Daring Greatly: How the Courage to Be Vulnerable Transforms the Way We Live, Love, Parent, and Lead*. New York: Gotham, 2012.

Brown, Brené. "The Power of Vulnerability." TED Talks, June 2010. Web. Date accessed: October 29, 2016. Available at: https://www.ted.com/talks/brene_brown_on_vulnerability?language=en.

Cain, Susan. *Quiet: The Power of Introverts in a World That Can't Stop Talking*. New York: Crown, 2012.

Cain, Susan. "The Power of Introverts." TED Talks. Date accessed: February 20, 2016. Available at: https://www.ted.com/talks/susan_cain_the_power_of_introverts?language=en.

Cameron, Julia. *The Artist's Way: A Spiritual Path to Higher Creativity*. 10th edn. Los Angeles, CA: Jeremy P. Tarcher/Putnam, 2002.

Chekhov, Anton Pavlovich, and Stephen Mulrine. *The Seagull*. London: Nick Hern, 1997.

Clark, David M., and Adrian Wells. "A Cognitive Model of Social Phobia." In Richard G. Heimberg (ed.), *Social Phobia: Diagnosis, Assessment, and Treatment* (pp. 69–93). New York: Guilford, 1995.

Cohen, Bonnie Bainbridge, Lisa Nelson, and Nancy Stark Smith. *Sensing, Feeling, and Action: The Experiential Anatomy of Body-mind Centering*. Northampton, MA: Contact Editions, 1993.

Cohen, Robert. *Acting One*. Palo Alto, CA: Mayfield Pub., 1984.

Cuddy, Amy. "Your Body Language Shapes Who You Are." TED Talks, June 2012. Web. Date accessed: October 29, 2016. Available at: https://www.ted.com/talks/amy_cuddy_your_body_language_shapes_who_you_are?language=en.

Delaney, Barry. Email interview. March 1, 2016.

DeSteno, David. *The Truth about Trust: How It Determines Success in Life, Love, Learning, and More.* New York: Hudson Street Press, New York, 2014.

Dweck, Carol S. *Mindset: The New Psychology of Success.* New York: Random House, 2006.

Ekman, Paul. *Emotions Revealed: Recognizing Faces and Feelings to Improve Communication and Emotional Life.* New York: Times, 2003.

Fisher, Steve. "The Ins and Outs of Onstage Intimacy." *NOW Toronto Magazine,* May 4, 2016. Web. Date accessed: June 13, 2016. Available at: https://nowtoronto.com/stage/theatre/the-ins-and-outs-of-onstage-intimacy/.

Foa, Edna B., and Michael J. Kozak. "Emotional Processing of Fear: Exposure to Corrective Information." *Psychological Bulletin,* vol. 99, no. 1 (1986): 20–35. Web. Date accessed: October 29, 2016. Available at: www.ufrgs.br/toc/images/artigos_de_interesse/Modelo%20cognitivo-comportamental/Emotional%20processing%20of%20fear%20Foa%201986.pdf.

Folino White, Ann. Email interview. February 25, 2015.

Folino White, Ann. Personal interview. Spring 2015.

Gallwey, W. Timothy. *The Inner Game of Tennis.* New York: Random House, 1974.

Gallwey, W. Timothy. *The Inner Game of Golf.* New York: Random House, 1981.

Gallwey, W. Timothy, and Bob Kriegel. *The Inner Game of Skiing.* London: Pan, 1987.

Goldin, Philippe R., Kateri Mcrae, Wiveka Ramel, and James J. Gross. "The Neural Bases of Emotion Regulation: Reappraisal and Suppression of Negative Emotion." *Biological Psychiatry 63.* 6 (2008): 577-86. Web.

Goeke, Sarah. Personal interview. Spring 2015.

Goldstein, Thalia R. Email interview. March 2, 2016.

Goldstein, Thalia R., and Paul Bloom. "The Mind on Stage: Why Cognitive Scientists Should Study Acting." *Trends in Cognitive Sciences,* vol. 15, no. 4 (2011): 141–2. Web. Date accessed: February 20, 2016. Available at: http://minddevlab.yale.edu/sites/default/files/files/The%20Mind%20on%20Stage%20GoldsteinBloomMindOnStageTiCS.pdf.

Green, Barry, and W. Timothy Gallwey. *The Inner Game of Music.* Garden City, NY: Anchor/Doubleday, 1986.

Greenbaum, Matthew. Personal interview. Fall 2015.

Greenberg, Leslie S. *Emotion-focused Therapy.* Washington, DC: American Psychological Association, 2011.

Gross, James J. *Handbook of Emotion Regulation.* New York: Guilford, 2007.

Hannaford, Carla. *Smart Moves: Why Learning Is Not All in Your Head.* Arlington, VA: Great Ocean, 1995.

Hayes, Steven C., Jason B. Luoma, Frank W. Bond, Akihiko Masuda, and Jason Lillis. "Acceptance and Commitment Therapy: Model, Processes and Outcomes." *Behaviour Research and Therapy,* vol. 44, no. 1 (2006): 1–25. Web. Date accessed: September 10, 2016. Available at: https://www.ncbi.nlm.nih.gov/pubmed/16300724.

Hopwood, Chris. Personal interview. Spring 2015.

Horvath, Adam O., and Leslie S. Greenberg. *The Working Alliance: Theory, Research, and Practice*. New York: Wiley, 1994.

Huston, Daniel. Personal interview. Spring 2015.

Isaacson, Rupert. *The Horse Boy: A Memoir of Healing*. New York: Back Bay, 2010.

Jackson, Joshua J., and Christopher J. Soto. "Five-Factor Model of Personality," *Oxford Bibliographies in Psychology* (2015). Available at Oxford Bibliographies Online: www.oxfordbibliographies.com/view/document/obo-9780199828340 /obo-9780199828340-0120.xml. Date accessed: February 20, 2016.

Jeffries, Stuart. "Inside the Mind of an Actor (literally)." *The Guardian*, November 23, 2009. Available at: www.theguardian.com/science/2009/nov/24 /fiona-shaw-neuroscience. Date accessed: February 20, 2016.

Jensen, Eric. *Teaching with Poverty in Mind: What Being Poor Does to Kids' Brains and What Schools Can Do about It*. Alexandria, VA: ASCD, 2009.

Jung, C. G. *Psychological Types; Or, The Psychology of Individuation*. London: Paul, Trench, Trubner, 1923.

Kabat-Zinn, Jon. *Wherever You Go, There You Are: Mindfulness Meditation in Everyday Life*. New York: Hyperion, 1994.

Kapit, Wynn, and Lawrence M. Elson. *The Anatomy Coloring Book*. New York: HarperCollins College, 1993.

Kashdan, Todd B., and Robert Biswas-Diener. *The Power of Negative Emotion: How Anger, Guilt and Self Doubt Are Essential to Success and Fulfillment*. London: Oneworld Publications, Richmond, 2015.

Kemp, Rick. *Embodied Acting: What Neuroscience Tells Us about Performance*. London: Routledge, 2012, pp. 130–1.

Kross, Ethan, and Ozlem Ayduk. "Making Meaning out of Negative Experiences by Self-Distancing." *Current Directions in Psychological Science*, vol. 20, no. 3 (2011): 187–91. Web. Date accessed: February 20, 2016. Available at: http:// cdp.sagepub.com/content/20/3/187.

Kross, Ethan, Emma Bruehlman-Senecal, Jiyoung Park, Aleah Burson, Adrienne Dougherty, Holly Shablack, Ryan Bremner, Jason Moser, and Ozlem Ayduk. "Self-talk as a Regulatory Mechanism: How You Do It Matters." *Journal of Personality and Social Psychology*, vol. 106, no. 2 (2014): 304–24. Web. Copyright 2014 American Psychological Association. Reproduced with permission.

Leary, Timothy. *Interpersonal Diagnosis of Personality; a Functional Theory and Methodology for Personality Evaluation*. New York: Ronald, 1957.

Letts, Tracy. *Bug: A Play*. Evanston, IL: Northwestern University Press, 2006.

McNiff, Shaun. *Trust the Process: An Artist's Guide to Letting Go*. 1st edn. Boston, MA: Shambhala, New York 1998.

McNiff, Shaun. *Imagination in Action: Secrets for Unleashing Creative Expression*. Boston, MA: Shambhala, New York, 2015.

Maxwell, Ian, Mark Seton, and Maryann Szabo. "The Australian Actors' Wellbeing Study: A Preliminary Report." *About Performance*, no. 13 (2015): 69–113. Web. Date accessed: February 20, 2016. Available at: www.questia.com/library/ journal/1P3-3833467261/the-australian-actors-wellbeing-study-a-preliminary.

Merceica, Melissa. Personal interview. Spring 2015.

Moser, Jason, PhD. Personal interview. Fall 2015.

Mischel, Walter. *The Marshmallow Test: Mastering Self-control.* New York: Little, Brown, 2014. Print.

Novello, Jonathon. Personal interview. Fall 2015.

Ramirez, G., and S. L. Beilock. "Writing about Testing Worries Boosts Exam Performance in the Classroom." *Science,* vol. 331., no. 6014 (2011): 211–13.

Reisberg, Marika. Personal interview. Fall 2015.

Roznowski, Rob. *Inner Monologue in Acting.* New York: Palgrave Macmillan, 2013.

Rūmī, Jalāl Al-Dīn. "The Guest House." *The Essential Rumi.* Trans. Coleman Barks. San Francisco, CA: Harper, 1996. Permission granted for use by translator.

Sacks, Oliver. *The Man Who Mistook His Wife for a Hat and Other Clinical Tales.* New York: Summit, 1985.

Savrami, Katia. "Does Dance Matter? The Relevance of Dance Technique in Professional Actor Training." *Research in Dance Education,* vol. 17, no. 2, (2016): 1–114. Web. Date accessed: July 14, 2016. Available at: http://www.tandfonline.com/doi/abs/10.1080/14647893.2016.1208647?scroll=top&needAccess=true&journalCode=crid20.

Scott, Sophie. "Why We Laugh." TED Talks, March 2015. Web. Date accessed: February 20, 2016. Available at: www.ted.com/talks/sophie_scott_why_we_laugh?language=en.

Seton, Mark. Email interview. February 25, 2015.

Shakespeare, William. *Twelfth Night; Or, What You Will.* New Haven, CT: Yale University Press, 1954.

Shapiro, Mel. *An Actor Performs.* Fort Worth, TX: Harcourt Brace College, 1997.

Sina, Tonia. "Intimate Encounters; Staging Intimacy and Sensuality." VCU Scholars Compass, n.d. Web. Date accessed: October 29, 2016. Available at: http://scholarscompass.vcu.edu/cgi/viewcontent.cgi?article=2070&context=etd.

Sullivan, Harry Stack. *The Interpersonal Theory of Psychiatry.* New York: Norton, 1953.

Taylor, Jane Vincent. *The Lady Victory: Poems.* Cincinnati, OH: Turning Point, 2012.

Tharp, Twyla, and Mark Reiter. *The Creative Habit: Learn It and Use It for Life: A Practical Guide.* New York: Simon & Schuster, 2003.

*The Horse Boy: A Father's Quest to Heal His Son.* Dir. Michael O. Scott. Roadshow, 2009.

van der Kolk, Bessel. *The Body Keeps the Score: Brain, Mind, and Body in the Healing of Trauma.* New York: Penguin, 2015.

Zinker, Joseph C. *Creative Process in Gestalt Therapy.* New York: Brunner/Mazel, 1977.

Please note that personal interviews were edited for clarity and succinctness.

# Index

Note: page numbers in **bold** indicate illustrations.